W9-BBQ-098

PRENTICE-HALL FOUNDATIONS OF F[illegible]

J. Fred Weston
The Scope and Methodology of Finance

Robert K. Jaedicke and Robert T. Sprouse
Accounting Flows: Income, Funds, and Cash

James T. S. Porterfield
Investment Decisions and Capital Costs

Ezra Solomon and Jaime C. Laya
Measuring Profitability

Alexander A. Robicheck and Stewart C. Myers
Optimal Financing Decisions

John C. Burton
The Management of Working Capital

Alan Coleman
The Financial Management of Financial Institutions

Herbert E. Dougall
Capital Markets and Institutions, Second Edition

Jack Clark Francis and Stephen H. Archer
Portfolio Analysis

James C. Van Horne
Function and Analysis of Capital Market Rates

Edwin J. Elton and Martin J. Gruber
Finance as a Dynamic Process

Baruch Lev
Financial Statement Analysis: A New Approach

Dileep R. Mehta
Working Capital Management

PRENTICE-HALL FOUNDATIONS OF FINANCE SERIES

Ezra Solomon, *Editor*

WORKING CAPITAL MANAGEMENT

Dileep R. Mehta
Georgia State University

DISCARDED

PRENTICE-HALL, INC., Englewood Cliffs, New Jersey

Library of Congress Cataloging in Publication Data

Mehta, Dileep R.
Working capital management.

Bibliography: p.
1. Working capital. I. Title.
HF5550.M515 658.1'5244 74-7417
ISBN 0-13-967539-6
ISBN 0-13-967521-3 (pbk.)

© 1974 by PRENTICE-HALL, INC., Englewood Cliffs, New Jersey
All rights reserved. No part of this book may be
reproduced in any form or by any means without
permission in writing from the publisher.

Printed in the United States of America

10 9 8 7 6 5 4 3 2 1

PRENTICE-HALL INTERNATIONAL, INC., London
PRENTICE-HALL OF AUSTRALIA, PTY. LTD., Sydney
PRENTICE-HALL OF CANADA, LTD., Toronto
PRENTICE-HALL OF INDIA PRIVATE LIMITED, New Delhi
PRENTICE-HALL OF JAPAN, Inc., Tokyo

Table of Contents

INTRODUCTION 1

I. Purpose—1. II. Characteristics of Working Capital—1. III. Management Practice—5. IV. Summary—7.

PART ONE: ACCOUNTS RECEIVABLE MANAGEMENT

I The Credit-Granting Decision 11

I. Introduction—11. II. The Conventional Approach—12. III. The Discriminant Analysis—14. IV. The Decision-Tree Approach—23. V. Control Measures—27. VI. Conclusion—31.

II Collection Measures and Their Effectiveness 33

I. Introduction—33. II. Selection of Collection Policy and Capital Budgeting—34. III. The Markov Process and Cash-flow Estimates—36. IV. Application—41. V. Conclusion—44.

III Credit Policy Integration 50

I. Introduction—50. II. Cost Estimates—51. III. The Set of Decision-rules—57. IV. Control Indices—63. V. Conclusion—67.

PART TWO: INVENTORY MANAGEMENT

IV Inventory Management Under Certainty **71**

I. Introduction—71. II. Relevant Costs—72. III. Basic Single-item Models—73. IV. Multi-item Considerations—91. V. Evaluation of the Inventory System—98. VI. Conclusion—100.

V Inventory System under Certainty **101**

I. Introduction—101. II. Safety Stock and the Fixed-order System—102. III. Safety Stock and the Fixed-period System—110. IV. Comparison of the Two Systems—117. V. The (s, S) System—118. VI. Control of Multi-item Inventories—124. VII. Conclusion—129.

PART THREE: CASH MANAGEMENT

VI Cash Management and Marketable Securities **133**

I. Introduction—133. II. Cash Management and Inventory Theory—135. III. Cash Balances and Portfolio Management—141. IV. Conclusion—145.

VII Cash Management and Working Capital: Integration through Programming Approaches **150**

I. Introduction—150. II. Wealth Maximization and Certainty—151. III. Linear Programming and Uncertainty—158. IV. Goal Programming—160. V. Conclusion—164.

VIII Cash as a Residual Asset and Stimulation **165**

I. Introduction—165. II. Simulation—166. III. Simulation and Decision-Making: Concluding Remarks—172.

REFERENCES **175**

INDEX **179**

Editor's Note

THE subject matter of Financial Management is in the process of rapid change. A growing analytical content, virtually nonexistent ten years ago, has displaced the earlier descriptive treatment as the center of emphasis in the field.

These developments have created problems both for teachers and students. On the one hand, recent and current thinking, which is addressed to basic questions that cut across traditional divisions of the subject matter, does not fit neatly into the older structure of academic courses and texts in Corporate Finance. On the other hand, the new developments have not yet stabilized and as a result have not yet reached the degree of certainty, lucidity, and freedom from controversy that would permit all of them to be captured within a single, straightforward treatment at the textbook level. Indeed, given the present rate of change, it will be years before such a development can be expected.

One solution to the problem, which the present Foundations of Finance Series tries to provide, is to cover the major components of the subject through short independent studies. These individual essays provide a vehicle through which the writer can concentrate on a single sequence of ideas and thus communicate some of the excitement of current thinking and controversy. For the teacher and student, the separate self-contained books provide up-to-date surveys of current thinking on each sub-area covered, and at the same time permit maximum flexibility in course and curriculum design.

EZRA SOLOMON

Preface

In this book I have tried to provide a conceptual foundation for managing working capital (or current assets). This analysis is founded on some reasonably observable characteristics of working capital components. Since I have been unable to devise (or find in the finance literature) any systematic and general treatment of current liability components on their own, and since I have found their inclusion in the definition of working capital ambiguous anyway, I have refrained from any extensive discussion of current liabilities. If the reader does not agree, I urge him to substitute the words "current assets" for "working capital" in this book, including its title.

The orientation of this book charts a course that avoids the two extremes of being axiomatic (where normative behavioral prescriptions are derived rigorously from a set of axioms) and institutional (where existing practices are described with a tacit assumption of their optimality). Instead, the book focuses on exploiting analytical apparatuses for operational efficiency of the finance manager. It is possible that such an approach may offend the aesthetics of the theoretician while, at the same time, turning off the practicioner looking for black boxes of behavioral rules. However, if the reader is either sufficiently intrigued by this book to create more general, abstract frameworks or encouraged enough to implement his modification of the frameworks provided here, my purpose in writing this book will be fully accomplished.

As to the prerequisite level of the student, basic calculus, some elementary linear algebra, and a familiarity with the rudimentary concepts of probability and statistics should prove adequate.

At times, discussion of the subject matter may seem complex, if not tedious. Terse treatment in these places has been avoided in order to facilitate matters for the reader who wants to verify the results or modify some premises for implementation. In general, complex derivations are placed either in the sections with asterisks (*), or in appendices at the end of chapters so that the reader may skip them without loss of continuity.

A variety of sources has provided many of the ideas appearing in this book. Wherever possible, I have acknowledged the contribution of specific sources. I beg the reader's indulgence for any omissions that may have crept in. However, I would be remiss if I failed to mention the enormous contribution of Victor Andrews, Charles Christenson, and Eli Shapiro in the development of some of the basic ideas for this work. During my graduate studies and thereafter, at one time or another, they patiently provided trenchant comments on an oft-cryptic piece of work. Eli Shapiro encouraged me in more than one way to undertake this book. His proddings and efforts have meant much more to me than words here can adequately express.

At various stages in the preparation of this book, I have also benefitted from the critical comments of Professors Rashad Abdel-Khalik, Harold Bierman, Michael Keenan, Ezra Solomon, and Gerard von Dohlen. Needless to say, they should not be held responsible for any remaining errors or inadequacies of the book, since I did not always follow their wise counsel.

Bill Firth, Michael Melody, and Tom Paul (now with Goodyear Publishing) of Prentice-Hall have been involved with the logistics of this book at one stage or another. Their efforts have been beyond the call of duty and are appreciated by the author.

Finally, my wife Allison often bore the brunt of the frustrating task of preparing this book. She not only typed the manuscript in its different draft forms, but also helped edit its contents.

Acknowledgements

The first part of the book on accounts receivable management is partly or substantially based on some of my work that appeared as journal articles. I wish to thank the editors of the following journals for allowing me to use the articles in this book:

Management Science (Chapter 1),
Decision Sciences (Chapter 2),
Journal of Financial and Quantitative Analysis (Chapter 3).

Dileep R. Mehta

Atlanta
February, 1974

Introduction

I. Purpose

THE purpose of this work is the construction of a set of rules for making operating decisions regarding working capital, which together with logically related control indices, will enable the manager to effectively evaluate both the rules—that is, the policy—and the lower management responsible for carrying out that policy.

II. Characteristics of Working Capital

A. Short Life Span

Components of current assets, or working capital,[1] consist of cash and marketable securities, accounts receivable, and inventories.[2] These asset forms are short-lived: typically, their life span does not exceed one year. In practice, however, some assets that violate this criterion are still classified as current assets. For example, United States government

[1] Some authors prefer to include both current assets and current liabilities in working capital. Since *net working capital* refers to the excess of current assets over current liabilities, we shall regard the terms *current assets* and *working capital* as synonymous.

[2] For convenience, prepaid expenses are lumped together with inventories.

obligations that are anticipated to be held until a maturity date exceeding one year are often lumped together with cash and marketable securities. Similarly, tobacco companies keep their raw materials in storage for more than a year, but nevertheless report these inventories as current assets.

B. Swift Transformation and Interrelated Asset Forms

In addition to their short span of life, current asset components have one other characteristic in common: each component is swiftly transformed into other asset forms. Thus, cash is utilized to replenish inventories; inventories are diminished when credit sales occur that augment accounts receivable; collection of accounts receivable increases the cash balances. The concept of this "cash cycle" is explored extensively in finance textbooks. There are two major implications concerning the managing of working capital that need elaboration. First, decisions that affect the level of working capital are frequent and repetitive. If the manager becomes too involved with the operating function, he will have little time to develop a broader perspective for efficient management. His function will be better served if he creates a framework of *unambiguous* rules for making routine decisions of this nature that are consistent with a set of goals and hands these rules down to lower management. At the same time the manager must set up some form of feedback to ensure proper adherence to these rules by lower management and to ascertain that proper implementation of the rules actually leads to the desired results. This feedback can be effectively provided by indices based upon aggregated information.

The second implication is that a close interaction among working-capital components entails the assumption that efficient management of one asset form cannot be undertaken without simultaneous consideration of other components. However, initially we will consider each asset form separately; this procedure may be justified on the following grounds:

1. It will enable us to concentrate on distinct economic characteristics of each asset form, thereby avoiding the trap of forcing onto all forms certain analytical frameworks appropriate only for one form. For instance, although there is a basic similarity between cash and inventories, simple inventory models are found to be inappropriate for cash management.
2. Indirect links among these asset forms are created through the concept of the cost of capital, as we shall see later.
3. Such a partial examination is operationally relevant, as long as a department (such as the credit department) is an entity and is held responsible for its goals. Thus, the credit department is directly concerned with the bad-debt experience and not, say, with the level of inventories; consequently, the credit manager is reluctant to extend credit to submarginal customers even when the resultant bad-debt cost estimate is less than the cost of excess inventories.

C. Asset Forms and Synchronization of Activity Levels

A third characteristic of working-capital components is that their life span depends upon the extent to which three basic activities—production, distribution (sales), and collection—are noninstantaneous and unsynchronized. If these three activities were instantaneous and synchronized, the management of working capital would obviously be a trivial proposition.[3] When the element of uncertainty is added to the lack of synchronization among these activities, the need for effective working capital management becomes even more intense. If production and sales were synchronized, there would be no need for inventories. Similarly, when all customers pay cash, management of accounts receivable becomes unnecessary. Even when these activities are not synchronized, the need for inventories and accounts receivable may be obviated by dovetailing production to customers' orders and accepting only those orders that are fully paid upon delivery of goods. However, such practices are unlikely to attract sufficient business for survival in a competitive economy.

To the extent that working-capital components affect and are affected by production, sales, and collection activities, a simultaneous consideration of the components and the activities is necessary. However, for the sake of convenience, initially we will regard one or more of these activities as exogenous, and thereby will only trace their *effects* on working capital. Later, our integration attempt would consider simultaneous determination of both asset forms and activity levels.

Since sales activities are pivotal in these interrelationships, the critical role of reasonably accurate sales forecasting in managing working capital cannot be overstressed. Methods of sales forecasting will not be described or prescribed in this work because conceptual generalizations are not possible. At this point, therefore, we may note only one significant aspect of sales forecasting in relation to the management of working capital. Liquidity crises are typically acute in the vicinity of turning points of the sales cycle. During the beginning of the recovery phase, the need for capacity expansion and modernization, as well as the build-up of accounts receivable and finished goods inventories, puts pressures on the available liquidity. In the aftermath of the downturn, liquidation of receivables provides a source of liquidity; but if the turning point is not correctly anticipated, resources tied up in inventories can lead to an embarrassing liquidity situation. Hence, determination of *timing* of turning points in the sales cycle is crucial for efficient management of working capital. For forecasting purposes, then, what we need is the lead-and-lag relationship whereby a turning point in one indicator warns us about the imminent turning point of our sales cycle. Needless to say, economic reasoning, which identifies

---

[3] Even though this lack of synchronization has been a focal point in the literature dealing with inventory management, it has received only perfunctory and peripheral attention in the finance literature.

such a lead-and-lag relationship, should ideally provide the basis for any such forecasting.

The role of synchronization of various asset forms and activities is also significant in behavioral terms. A current asset component, by providing linkage, can be viewed as an extension of two activities. Thus, both marketing and production managers have an interest in inventories, or both marketing and credit managers are concerned with collection policies. However, their concerns may not be similar. Even when different departments agree upon a set of goals, their priorities may differ. For instance, both marketing and production managers may agree that satisfied customers and elimination of idle machine capacity are desirable goals, but the marketing manager's preference for product differentiation for a wider market may be opposed by the production manager on the ground that machine set-up costs would be excessive. The finance manager may exhibit still different priorities. He may regard a higher inventory turnover essential for effective bargaining for funds. Whether this is actually the case in particular instances is immaterial. The essential point is that the viewpoint of the finance manager does not necessarily coincide with that of the other managers who have a direct interest in the asset components we are considering in this study.[4] Needless to say, in this book we shall adopt the viewpoint of the finance manager.[5]

The essence of the finance manager's viewpoint is the efficient raising and allocation of financial resources of the firm.[6] Such a viewpoint has several implications for the management of working capital. First, given the short life span of working-capital components, the distinction between profit and wealth (incorporating the concept of discounting over time) will not be significant, especially when static models are considered. Second, the efficient *raising* of funds for short durations (represented as "liabilities" on the balance sheet) will be considered only during the integration phase, given our definition of working capital. Third, we will rely on the standard of the *cost of capital* to ensure efficient management of *individual* current asset components. This emphasis on the cost of capital suggests that the out-of-pocket costs, such as the interest amount on loans, would not be relevant as investment costs. One theoretical issue involved in the use of the cost of capital should be pointed out: this concept embodies not only time preference but also the attitude of the investor regarding risk. Since

---

[4] It is interesting to note that the literature dealing with inventory management has the viewpoint of the production manager, as Beranek [1966] has noted. Thus the cost-minimization objective (with lip service to the lost sales cost) is rarely constrained by funds availability.

[5] To the extent that these viewpoints conflict, one or the other may prevail in practice—the matter will be settled by the bargaining strength of the various parties involved. It is then necessary that the finance manager know all his cards in order to play the game skillfully.

[6] A succinct rationale for this statement is provided by Solomon [1963].

different working-capital components have different risk potentials, it does not seem reasonable to use the *same* measure for all these components. One way to determine different cutoff rates for asset forms with different risk potentials is through considerations connected with portfolio analysis.[7] However, the critical problem in this case is the basic inconsistency between the static nature of the portfolio theory and the need for a dynamic framework for management of working capital. Dynamic transformations of the portfolio theory invoke assumptions that make them useless for this purpose. For instance (as will be suggested in Chapter 8), the interrelationships among working-capital components make it necessary to undertake the complex task of convoluted distributions *over time* that are assumed away in portfolio analysis encompassing several periods.[8] For simplicity and convenience, then, the notion of risk will be assumed to be adequately reflected in the expected value[9] of cashflows and the conventional notion of the cost of capital (the risk-adjusted discount rate),[10] as far as the treatment of individual components is concerned.

The extent to which the proposed analysis applies may vary with the size of the operation. In small firms, it is likely that differences in viewpoints among different departments such as those suggested above do not exist. This may simplify the process of management, but it certainly would not obviate the need for managing working capital. Even in a small organization, at least one person is likely to evaluate performance on the basis of aggregated information, and at least one person has to consider distinct, conflicting viewpoints of production, marketing, and finance functions that bear upon working capital.

III. Management Practice

Management typically relies on rules of thumb, such as ratio measures, in order to delegate decision making at operating levels and to gauge the efficiency with which resources are allocated. These standards are derived from the firm's past experience or the average behavior of the industry to which the firm belongs. Violation of these

[7] See Tuttle and Litzenberger [1968] or Mehta [1974] for elaboration on this issue.

[8] See, for instance, Mossin [1968].

[9] Since working-capital components are short-lived, and transactions affecting them are frequent and repetitive, we may safely assume the validity of the law of large numbers: i.e., "After a large number of trials, the observed frequency will [not be likely] to diverge widely from probability" [Massé, 1962, p. 208]. This law, in turn, implies that risk is adequately reflected in the expected value or the first moment of the probability distribution of the economic process. Since the portfolio theory approach is justified on the relevance of the second and higher moments of the probability distribution, its across-the-board applicability to the management of working capital is dubious.

[10] Theoretical considerations, such as the effect of dividend or debt policy on the cost of capital, will not be considered here. Of course, the Modigliani-Miller hypothesis [1958, 1963] provides one benchmark in this instance.

standards calls for review and action by management.[11] For instance, inventory or receivable turnover ratio and current or acid-test ratio are utilized to detect overinvestment in working-capital components.

A major problem with these measures has been that control indices are not necessarily consistent with the operating rules delegated to lower management for routine decisions. For instance, it is hard to see why credit extension to firms with current ratios in excess of 2.5 and collection expenditures of $X per year should result in a ratio of sales to accounts receivable above a desirable number. Moreover, these measures suffer from limitations imposed by two underlying assumptions: (1) that historical experience is the true analog of efficiency, and (2) that the efficiency path is linear; that is, if a firm's bad-debt ratio standard is 1 percent, it holds true no matter what the *level* of sales or its *rate* of change may be. The validity of the second assumption is questionable in light of the fact that businesses often have variable, and at times discontinuous, growth rates. When these growth rates are translated into various forms of assets, each investment rate may exhibit a lead-and-lag tendency without being consistent over time. The first assumption is also questionable: historical experience in itself is not useless, but where it is relied upon exclusively, its deficiency cannot be overcome even by the use of seemingly more complex (but essentially mechanical) mathematical techniques.

It is not my intention to suggest that theorists should reprimand businessmen for relying exclusively on inadequate measures or even that businessmen are thoroughly content with the use of these measures. On the contrary, changes in economic conditions are often implicitly taken into account for evaluation, and decisions made at lower levels are explicitly modified by higher echelons to account for an uneven impact of growth rates on investment in different asset forms. However, the practice of explicit or implicit modification by higher echelons has become increasingly difficult in large companies that are developing into complex entities. As a result, policy makers are so far removed from decision makers that they are not likely to observe the details and intangible aspects of implementation that contribute greatly to the success or failure of policies.

We should note here that ratio measures in themselves are not necessarily deficient. It is only that the decision standards that are delegated —or the control standards against which these measures are assessed —may be inconsistent, arbitrary, or unreasonable. Our task is to provide analytical tools that can forge consistent, comprehensive, and definite standards. The urgency of the need for such tools becomes overwhelming in the face of the growing organizational complexity that is evident in the widening gap between decision makers and those who are responsible for the consequences of their decisions.

[11] Management concern over these standards also stems from the fact that superiors (board of directors), investors, and outsiders (creditors) often evaluate management in terms of these measures.

IV. Summary

The subject of working capital will be dealt with from the viewpoint of the financial manager of a large corporation. He is not involved with routine operating decisions dealing with cash, receivables, or inventories, but he is supposed to know whether resources invested in these asset forms are efficiently utilized. Rules of thumb, such as ratio measures, have often been found effective for such purpose, particularly when they are formed and utilized in the light of the finance manager's experience. However, these rules of thumb are considered deficient in two ways: (1) they do not have the directional flexibility necessary in a dynamic environment; and (2) their relationship to operating decision rules is at best tangential.

The goal of this work is to create a framework of less ambiguous decision-making rules (handed down to lower management for routine decisions) and logically interrelated control indices that enable the manager to evaluate policies and to take action on the basis of aggregated information.

In the following chapters we will initially treat each working capital component separately. Modelling is the main analytical vehicle; however, operational aspects of managerial problems are also introduced wherever it is feasible. The treatment primarily emphasizes dynamic models, but where necessary, static models are employed to facilitate the task of building dynamic models. The last two chapters explore some programming and heuristic techniques for an integration that encompasses simultaneous determination not only of resource allocation but also of activity levels.

Part One

ACCOUNTS RECEIVABLE MANAGEMENT

CREDIT policy measures consist of credit-granting and collection activities. Credit *granting* focuses on the choice of alternative asset forms of inventories and accounts receivable. Similarly, *collection* measures reflect the desirability of having assets in the form of cash or accounts receivable. Thus, credit policy affects the aggregate level of investment in accounts receivable as opposed to other current asset forms. The central issue revolves around what should be the level of receivables in the firm and to what extent deviations from this level are acceptable. Since the level of receivables is primarily affected by sales, it is generally referred to in relation to sales.

For control purposes, there is a need for standards indicating not only the right *quantity* but also the right magnitude of *risk* (reflected, for instance, in bad-debt estimates) that this quantity embodies. However, a *lower* level of receivables, incorporating *ceteris paribus* less risk, implies efficient policy implementation only in a limited sense. Stringent credit granting and rigorous collection measures, showing quantity- and quality-oriented indices well within standards, may adversely affect a firm's goodwill and future sales. In order to detect this undesirable effect, a third set of indices, which incorporates in some manner *lost sales estimates,* is necessary.

Chapter 1 deals with the formulation of credit-granting policy; Chapter 2 deals with selection of optimal collection measures, given the framework of a credit-granting policy; Chapter 3 integrates these two related phases of credit policy.

Credit is extended to a firm or to an individual. Credit extended by a nonfinancial firm to another firm is defined as *trade credit*. Credit extended to an individual is generally classied as *consumer credit*. The focus of this work will be on trade credit, because, due to certain institutional characteristics, the treatment of trade credit differs from that of consumer credit. First, trade credit generally involves credit to corporate bodies that have limited liability and a life span independent of that of individuals owning or controlling them. Second, demand for trade credit is fairly sensitive to changes in interest rate, whereas the demand for consumer credit is likely to be affected by changes in income or employment levels. These and other distinctive characteristics affect the investigation and collection procedures not only directly but also indirectly through different relative costs and benefits.

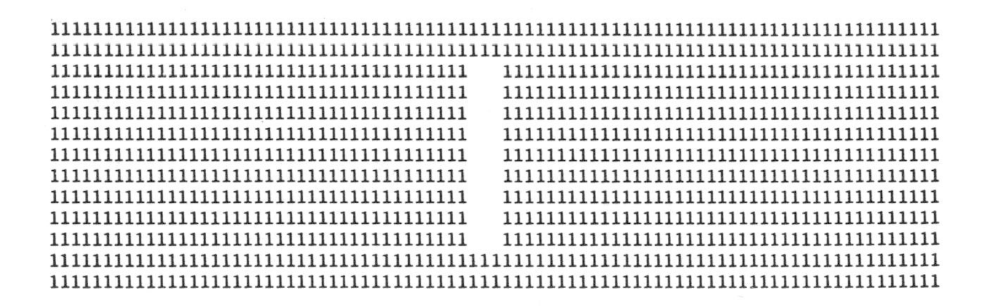

The Credit-Granting Decision

I. Introduction

CREDIT granting is essentially a sales tool facilitating customers' purchases. It is valuable to customers who cannot borrow from other sources and is appealing to customers who can borrow but find it cumbersome to do so. From a somewhat different perspective, credit granting enables customers to synchronize their sources and uses of funds to some extent.

From a credit manager's viewpoint, routine decisions underlying the credit policy are as follows:

1. When a request for credit arrives, should credit be granted?
2. If the credit request is acceptable, for what amount is it safe to grant credit?
3. Should the applicant be offered the incentive of a cash discount for early payments?
4. What collection measures are appropriate for a delinquent customer?

These four decisions are related and affect (1) the sales level, (2) collection cost and bad-debt losses, and (3) the form of investment (i.e., inventories, accounts receivable, and cash).

The first two decisions are significant because they influence subsequent phases of credit policy. Consequently, the initial "credit extension" phase is pivotal in the sense that management exercises its discretion primarily during this phase. The third decision, the size and availability of a cash discount, is generally determined by industry practices; deviation from these practices usually entails reprisals from competitors, low profit margins, or both. Finally, once the request for credit is approved and credit is granted, collection measures (or their absence) directly affect both the level of current investment in receivables and future requests for credit.

This chapter analyzes the credit-granting phase, considering other aspects of credit policy (particularly collection measures) as given. Attention is focused on formulating a framework for making decisions on individual credit requests and on measuring the impact of such a framework. In measuring this aggregate impact, the discussion is centered on control or evaluation indices designed to measure the impact of credit-granting policies on the level of sales, accounts receivable investment, and collection cost. The conventional treatment of the subject is briefly sketched in order to provide a perspective for the subsequent discussion of the two analytical techniques: discriminant analysis and the decision-tree approach.

Chapter 2 deals with the impact of collection measures on a firm's cash flows and investment in receivables. The analytical process in Chapter 2 differs from that of the present chapter in two respects. First, in Chapter 2 the credit-extension phase is assumed to be known and given; here, on the other hand, it is the collection-measures phase that is assumed to be known and constant. Second, a dynamic framework is utilized in Chapter 2, whereas only static frameworks are used here. These two partial analyses for the phases of credit extension and collection measures serve as building blocks for the integration to be made in Chapter 3, in order to account for their interactions.

Determination of cash discount policy will not be undertaken here because, as noted above, deviations from industry practices may have only short-lived advantages resulting as they do in competitive reprisals and low profit margins. Moreover, often only an insignificant number of customers take advantage of cash discounts, or the sales volume is insensitive to a change in the cash discount. In that case, a change in the cash discount affects only the profit (or contributions) margin, and the proposed frameworks are flexible enough to handle alternative cash discount policies. Finally, even when the sales volume is sensitive to cash discounts, the impact of a change in the cash discount is virtually similar to that of a change in price; hence, the standard economic analysis of price elasticity of demand may be useful in this instance.

II. The Conventional Approach

In assessing the risk of a request for credit, "three C's" are held to be relevant: *c*haracter, *c*apital, and *c*apacity.[1] Occasionally, two other

[1] Weston and Brigham [1972], p. 536. One of the most comprehensive works representing the conventional treatment is by Beckman [1962].

variables are added: *c*ollaterals and *c*onditions. The first factor, character, is supposed to measure the applicant's *willingness* to pay; the remaining factors should reflect his *ability* to pay. These factors are ranked qualitatively. A request for credit from an account having previous dealings with the firm is granted almost automatically, unless the request is for a significantly larger amount than usual, or the previous collection experience with the account leaves something to be desired, or business conditions have changed extensively since the previous transaction. Thus, attention is given primarily to requests for *initial* granting of credit.

Credit investigation is based on various sources of information. A typical list of these sources would include: other creditors' experience, financial reports, bankers' references, and Dun & Bradstreet reports. Ranking of sources, or their relative utility, is left to the credit manager's discretion.

Credit limits for an account are determined in the same way. Often, in addition, the applicant's annual requirement and debt-paying power are explicitly considered.

Credit terms offered to an acceptable account generally depend upon classification of the account into one of several predetermined risk categories, but they are also influenced by changes in such factors as inventory turnover, terms of competitive suppliers, the phase of the business cycle, the character of the commodity, the quantity of sales involved, and the nature of the credit risk.

Three major measures are suggested to top management for the evaluation of credit policies: (1) the ratio of bad debts to credit sales, (2) "turnover," or the ratio of credit sales to the level of receivables, and (3) aging of accounts. If the credit management is effective, the bad-debt ratio will not exceed a "ceiling standard," and the turnover ratio will not go below a "floor standard." When these standards are violated, review and action by management is called for. As far as aging of accounts is concerned, no such simple standards are applicable. However, a trend toward heavier concentration of receivables investment in remote past periods should be a signal for attention by management.

The conventional approach gives the credit manager an excellent opportunity to acquaint himself with effective procedures for treating a specific account. However, if this approach is followed, factors influencing a specific decision are analyzed in a vague, general way. Our interest is in delegating to lower management an unambiguous, rational policy framework in which routine decisions can be made. The conventional approach, at best, relies upon trial-and-error methods and experience gained from them to arrive at an effective set of rules for decision making.

A more serious problem lies in the lack of effective control measures corresponding to such a set of rules. The overall conventional control measures leave something to be desired. Apart from the general limitations of ratio measures (mentioned in the Introduction of the book), the evaluatory ratio measures employed in the conventional framework are defective for the following reasons. A bad-debt ratio, which is lower than the standard, or a higher turnover ratio, seems to indicate efficient credit management. However, these measures may not reflect the cost of forfeited goodwill (or lost sales) resulting from stringent collection measures or rigorous credit screening. In addition, the bad-debt ratio measures *current* bad-debt experience and *current* credit sales. Thus, it would be an inaccurate index to the extent that bad-debt experience reflects errors in judgment with respect to *past* credit sales. This inaccuracy would be particularly critical for firms with cyclical businesses. During prosperity, inefficiency in credit granting would be masked by increasing credit sales; the reverse would be true during a downturn.

In summary, the conventional approach, at best, is useful but indeterminate. At worst, it is misleading and disastrous. Given this inadequacy, statistical measures are proposed in the literature for credit-granting decisions. One of these measures is the discriminant analysis, which we shall now discuss in detail.

III. Discriminant Analysis

The "credit worthiness" of a request is a *qualitative* assessment, but in order to make this assessment a credit manager has to take into account *quantitative* factors or indicators. Since he cannot rely on any one factor exclusively, he has to assign weights to various indicators, either explicitly or implicitly, in light of his own experience and judgment. This procedure is satisfactory only as long as the number of incoming, or new, requests for credit is small. Once this number becomes large, the credit manager finds it increasingly difficult to judge individual requests adequately or consistently. Then it is a sound practice to delegate routine credit decisions to his subordinates. If these subordinates are not provided with a set of unambiguous rules for making decisions, they will have to rely upon their own judgment. This situation would entail not only tight control measures but also continually close supervision with the effect that delegation of authority becomes self-defeating. Obviously, a more desirable practice is to develop a consistent, unambiguous system that leaves little to subordinates' judgments. One great advantage of such a system is that it is effective even when less specialized personnel are in charge of decision making. Hence, in brief, what the manager requires is a technique that discriminates between good and poor risks. Since he is dealing with the uncertain future, and therefore must rely on statistical measures, the best procedure would be one that minimizes the cost of misclassification.

A statistical technique commonly advocated is the discriminant analysis.[2] Under this method, a variety of characteristics belonging to

[2] Nonparametric tests are also possible for screening the credit applicants. However, to my knowledge, the sampling properties of these methods are as yet not clearly established.

a sample of accounts that are satisfactory credit risks are compared with the corresponding characteristics of a sample of delinquent accounts. It is believed that the payment behavior of customers is systematically related to their observable attributes. The comparison enables one to select significant characteristics and assign them proper weights in order to design an index or quantitative measure. This index is subjected to additional statistical techniques to provide a cutoff value (or values) for decision making.

The manager, therefore, faces four tasks:

1. Determining significant factors.
2. Selecting the sample.
3. Assigning weights to factors in order to develop an index.
4. Establishing cutoff values for the index.

A. Significant Factors

Management judgment plays a critical role in the initial selection of a set of significant factors. For trade credit, the following set of indicators is commonly used: adequate liquidity or efficient use of working capital; stability and size of profitability; leverage; and the size of the firm. Other factors, such as the average age of management or resale value of the plant and equipment, are sometimes used; this usually happens when the request constitutes a significant portion of the applicant's total requirements, or a large amount in absolute terms. Even though the list of factors can be flexible, certain guidelines should be observed in preparing such a list.

First of all, it should be recognized that management judgment may not necessarily be totally reliable. Smith [1964], for instance, pointed out that even though credit managers attached great importance to the ratio of installment payment to monthly income, this factor ranked very low in statistical tests for consumer credit decisions.

Second, a set of factors under observation should be independent in a statistical (and economic) sense.[3] For instance, the ratio of current liability to inventory (indicating "free" inventories) and the ratio of inventory to *net* working capital (for excess- or under-stock situations) may be highly correlated. The practice of using both would attach excessive weights to a class of indicators and lead to an unreliable discriminant index in the end. A corollary to this requirement is that an indicator that is composed of independent characteristics may not be desirable; in such a case, two indicators may involve common characteristics, and thereby introduce a bias. For example, instability in *net* earnings is a result of both business and financial risks. A use of leverage in terms of debt-equity ratio would also involve the financial

[3] Statistical tests of correlation coefficients (for linear relationship) or non-parametric tests, such as quantile or the corner-association tests, may be applied to ensure independence.

risk. In this case, reliance on the instability of net earnings may prove to be misleading.

Third, all indicators should be quantitative. Even though a qualitative factor can be expressed on a quantitative scale, this is not desirable. For instance, the "character" of the applicant could be quantified in order to be used in the statistical analysis, but the quantification would call for subjective judgment on the part of subordinates. If these subordinates are capable of making effective decisions in this area, their talents are being wasted on routine decision making. If they are incapable, there is a potential for error in their judgment, and this defeats the purpose of delegating decision-making authority.

B. Selection of the Sample

In the selection of the sample, two issues must be dealt with:

1. What should be the size of the sample?
2. How should it be selected?

There are no hard and fast rules regarding the actual number of observations in the sample; however, the size of the sample should be large enough to ensure the reliability of the estimates.[4] In general, the larger the number of indicators (independent characteristics), the larger should be the size of the sample. Furthermore, as we shall see later, we determine the weights of the indicators on the basis of one part of the sample and test the applicability of the index on the remaining observations of the sample. Thus, the sample will be divided into two parts: the first part, to build the model; and the hold-out sample to test its effectiveness. This suggests that the sample should be roughly twice the size required for the reliability of estimates.

A sample can be selected in a variety of ways. We will consider here only three of them. In the first method, the sample is drawn from two sources: accounts written off as bad debts[5] and accounts that have exhibited acceptable payment behavior in the past. This method is the least expensive. However, it has the following drawbacks. It requires that observations in the sample contain full information on all relevant indicators; this may not necessarily be the case. Furthermore, results of the statistical analysis may prove unreliable if caution is not exercised against a potential source of bias. These observations come

---

[4] Indicators should have normal distributions within each classification group, as Williams [1959, p. 176] has noted. Thus requisites of normality would dictate the size of the sample.

[5] When there are few bad customers or comparatively few unacceptable applicants, it is difficult to obtain a reliable statistical profile of a bad customer. In such a case, we may deliberately select a larger proportion of bad debts than is usual. However, we should take a precaution against "over-representing" bad debts, so that the index cutoff may not be biased.

from the population of customers rather than the population of applicants. And because some credit applications in the past have been rejected outright, the bad-debt accounts selected for the sample will have already been subjected to a screening system. To that extent, indicators that otherwise might have proved strong discriminators may now be less significantly represented in the index.

A second method tries to overcome the bias in the first method by including not only accepted requests but also applications that were rejected during the relevant time period. Since actual experience is not available on the rejected applications, a subjective estimate is substituted for experience. This approach comes closer to observing the population of applicants rather than customers, but such estimates are unlikely to be the same as actual experience.

A third method involves granting credit to *all* randomly selected credit requests in a predetermined period, and then observing their behavior over time. Conceptually, this is the most desirable of the three methods; but the cost and time involved in formulating accurate estimates may prove to be prohibitive. For instance, if a firm recognizes a bad debt upon nonpayment within six months of credit extension, it will have to observe payment behavior for six months before it can classify an account as a bad debt. Of course, there are efficient techniques for extrapolating the experience of, say, one month that provide information on good and bad customers (we will have more to say about this matter in Chapters 2 and 3).

C. Construction of the Index

Discriminant analysis enables us to determine weights of different indicators in a manner similar to the regression analysis.[6] A simple illustration is provided to show how a discriminant index is devised.

Suppose a credit manager regards the following two variables as reliable indicators of accounts receivable behavior:

X_1 = the acid-test ratio, i.e., (cash + receivables/current liability)

X_2 = the inventory-turnover ratio, i.e., (sales/inventory)

We want to determine weights for X_1 and X_2; that is, the values of a and b in

[6] In the discriminant analysis, the dependent variable takes only discrete values such as quality of an account defined as either good or bad. On the other hand, the regression analysis assumes that the dependent variable had a continuous distribution. This distinction is often interpreted to mean that the discriminant analysis assumes two (or more) distinct populations, whereas the regression analysis is based on the assumption of a single, homogeneous population.

$$Y = aX_1 + bX_2$$

where $Y =$ the discriminant index

We selected 400 random requests during a month, and extended outright credit to all requests on a net-30-day basis. At the time credit was granted, we recorded values of the pertinent variables mentioned above. We observed the payment behavior of these accounts for the next three months. Accounts paid in full during this period were classified as "good risk" accounts. The remaining accounts were classified as "unacceptable." From this data, Tables 1–1 and 1–2 were prepared on the basis of 200 observations comprising the initial sample.

TABLE 1–1 Means and Difference between Means

	Good Risk	Unacceptable	Difference
Size	$n_1 = 150$	$n_2 = 50$	
$\overline{X}_{1i} = \sum X_{1i}/n_i$	1.2	0.9	0.3
$\overline{X}_{2i} = \sum X_{2i}/n_i$	10.5	9.0	1.5

TABLE 1–2 Data for Covariance Matrix

	Good Risk	Unacceptable	Sum
$\sum(X_{1i} - \overline{X}_{1i})^2$	70	15	85
$\sum(X_{2i} - \overline{X}_{2i})^2$	427	120	547
$\sum(X_{1i} - \overline{X}_{1i})(X_{2i} - \overline{X}_{2i})$	480	220	700

Note that the third column in Table 1–1 denotes differences between mean values for each of the two variables. We will define these quantities by the symbols D_1 and D_2, respectively. Similarly, the third column in Table 1–2 contains the sum of the first two columns, which in turn represent squared deviations from the mean (first two rows) and the product of deviations from the mean. Let us define S_{11}, S_{22}, and S_{12} to represent the quantities in the third column.

Now to solve for a and b, we construct two equations:

$$(1) \quad S_{11}a + S_{12}b = D_1$$

$$(2) \quad S_{12}a + S_{22}b = D_2$$

or,

$$85a + 700b = 0.3$$

$$700a + 547b = 1.5$$

Resolution of these two simultaneous equations gives us

$$a = 0.354 \qquad b = 0.033$$

Thus, $$Y = 0.354X_1 + 0.033X_2$$

Our construction of the index suggests that in our experience the acid-test ratio of the applicant is roughly ten times more significant than inventory-turnover ratio for determining his credit worthiness.

D. Cutoff Value

We now want to determine the effectiveness of the discriminant analysis. Suppose that applicants either pay within the acceptable time period, and thus are "good," *or* do not pay in time, and thus are "bad," with no grey region between these two categories. For this purpose, we may apply the weight .354 to the acid-test ratio and .033 to the inventory-turnover ratio for each applicant in the *hold-out* sample. We rank these applicants in a descending order of their index values and also record whether in fact they turned out to be good or bad. This procedure gives us the following information in condensed form:

TABLE 1–3

Index Value	Proportion of Good	Proportion of Bad
.00 – .62	0	0.75
.62 – .87	0.30	0.25
.87 and above	0.70	0

Thus we find that an index value above 0.87 indicates a good applicant, whereas an index value below 0.62 indicates a bad applicant. However, in the range between 0.62 and 0.87 good and bad applicants overlap. The usefulness of the discriminant analysis can now be appreciated. In this inconsistent range we have now 30 percent of the good applicants and 25 percent of the bad applicants. Above or below this range, credit-granting decisions can be made outright; within the inconsistent range, they can be made by either the manager or some skilled credit analyst. This procedure reduces the load of the credit manager, but he can devise a still better procedure by combining the Bayesian analysis with the appropriate cost information in the following manner.

Suppose the manager has found from his experience that 90 percent of the credit requests are good and 10 percent are bad. He also knows that for every dollar of credit sales, \$0.40 represents contribution margin and \$0.60 variable cost.

The manager now transforms the information given in Table 1–3 into a cumulative form, and at the same time divides the inconsistent range—the values between 0.62 and 0.87—in such a way as to obtain the cumulative frequencies of bad and good applicants at the interval of 0.01 of the index value. In this way, he produces the following information:

Index Value (less than)	Cumulative Proportion of Good Requests	Cumulative Proportion of Bad Requests
0.62	0	0.75
0.63	0	0.77
	...	
0.75	0.1	0.95
	...	
0.86	0.30	1.00
0.87	0.30	1.00
⋮	⋮	⋮

Such a presentation can be interpreted as follows: 10 percent of the good applicants and 95 percent of the bad applicants have an index value not larger than 0.75. In a concise form,

$$\text{Prob}\ (I_{0.75} \mid \text{Good}) = 0.10$$

$$\text{Prob}\ (I_{0.75} \mid \text{Bad}) = 0.95$$

This is read as "the probability is .10 that an applicant has the score 0.75 or less, given our knowledge of his being good." Now, the Bayes theorem suggests that

$$\begin{aligned}\text{Prob}\ (\text{Good} \mid I_{0.75}) &= \frac{\text{Prob}\ (\text{Good } \textit{and } I_{0.75})}{\text{Prob}\ (I_{0.75})} \\ &= \frac{\text{Prob}\ (I_{0.75} \mid \text{Good})\ \text{Prob}\ (\text{Good})}{\text{Prob}\ (I_{0.75} \mid \text{Good})\ \text{Prob}\ (\text{Good}) + \text{Prob}\ (I_{0.75} \mid \text{Bad})\ \text{Prob}\ (\text{Bad})}\end{aligned}$$

Thus, with Prob (Good) = 0.9 and Prob (Bad) = 0.1, we get

$$\begin{aligned}\text{Prob}\ (\text{Good} \mid I_{0.75}) &= \frac{(0.1)(0.9)}{(0.1)(0.9) + (0.95)(0.1)} \\ &= \frac{0.09}{0.09 + 0.095} = 0.49\end{aligned}$$

Since, by assumption, an applicant can be either good or bad,

$$\text{Prob}\ (\text{Good} \mid I_{0.75}) + \text{Prob}\ (\text{Bad} \mid I_{0.75}) = 1,$$

$$\text{Prob}\ (\text{Bad} \mid I_{0.75}) = 0.51$$

Thus when the index value for an applicant is equal to or less than 0.75, the likelihood that he will be good is 0.49. What we have done here is to combine the manager's valuable experience (that 90 percent of the requests are good and 10 percent of them are bad) with the results of the experiment on the hold-out sample. This enabled us to obtain the probability of payment (likelihood of being good) for an applicant with a specific index value. We can now combine this likelihood estimate with the cost estimate and the size of the credit request. If an applicant requests credit for $X, and has the index value 0.75, the probability of payment is 0.49. If he is refused credit, the 40 percent contribution margin on $X will be lost, and the *lost sales cost* will be

(Contribution margin) (Credit amount) (Probability of payment)

or $$.196X$$

On the other hand, if he is granted credit, and subsequently does not pay, the variable cost will be incurred by the firm. Thus the *acceptance cost* will be

(Variable cost) (Credit amount) (Probability of nonpayment)

or $$0.306X$$

We find, then, that the acceptance cost is larger than the rejection cost when an applicant has an index value equal to or below 0.75. Hence, such an applicant should *not* be granted credit.

When we undertake similar analyses for index values 0.76, 0.77, etc., we will have a more precise value for the index below which all credit requests are rejected. The advantage of such a procedure is clear. We are likely to have a precise cutoff value for granting credit. Even if that does not occur, we will have a much smaller "inconsistent range" where granting or refusing credit may be a matter of indifference; thus only for this range would decisions be made by the credit manager. For instance, we may find such a range in our example given by the values 0.81 to 0.83. The Bayesian analysis and the cost information have, then, enabled the manager to reduce his personal evaluation of requests from the number contained in the range 0.63–0.87 to the much smaller number contained in the range 0.81–0.83.

It may happen that the initial "inconsistent range" is too wide to be acceptable, i.e., the discriminant function is not effective; or we may want to know whether an additional variable would provide even better discrimination. In this case, the following procedure may be adopted.

Suppose that our index is now

$$Y = aX_1 + bX_2 + cX_3.$$

We find the values for a, b, and c in the same fashion as before.[7] We apply the procedure to the hold-out sample as it was applied above in the two-indicator case and judge whether the resultant "inconsistent range" is smaller than before.

E. Evaluation

The discriminant analysis enables us to take advantage of the credit manager's experience and insight regarding the relevant indicators of an applicant's "credit worthiness." At the same time, it enables us to provide objective weights for these indicators if they are effective. This is particularly useful for delegating responsibility for routine decisions to lower management because little judgment is called for in the application of these decision-making rules.

One major drawback of the discriminant analysis, however, is that in its conventional form it may be an economically unsound system. Collection of information costs time and money. Often, the effort is not worthwhile. However, the discriminant analysis does not discriminate against such effort. Suppose that a request for credit from a new account is for a small amount, say \$50. If the profit is going to be \$6, it is hardly worthwhile to spend \$7 on collecting and processing a variety of financial data. Moreover, it is doubtful whether collecting relevant information for extending credit to such firms as General Motors is worthwhile. Of course, these cases may be extreme examples. But the question remains: Where do we draw the line? In other words, we need to determine what information is pertinent for a variety of situations.

We may choose to leave this task to the discretion of lower management. But then we will be defeating our own purpose—to hand down unambiguous decision-making rules. Moreover, if members of lower management are capable of sound judgment in such matters, perhaps their competence is being wasted on routine decisions.

One operational caveat of the discriminant analysis cannot be overemphasized. As was noted earlier, this analysis requires *quantitative* indicators (not so much for statistical reasons as for organizational purposes because measuring qualitative factors on a subjective, cardinal scale is possible but is likely to inject unqualified judgments of lower management into the analysis). Some firms often introduce quantitative indicators even when these indicators increase the danger of a bias of

---

[7] Specifically, a three-variable model would require

1. Computation of a third row $\overline{X}_{3i}$ in Table 1–1.
2. Computation of three additional rows in Table 1–2 dealing with the quantities $\sum(X_{3i} - \overline{X}_{3i})^2$, $\sum(X_{1i} - \overline{X}_{1i})(X_{3i} - \overline{X}_{3i})$, and $\sum(X_{2i} - \overline{X}_{2i})(X_{3i} - \overline{X}_{3i})$ in order to derive S_{33}, S_{13}, and S_{23}, respectively.
3. A solution of three simultaneous equations

$$\sum_{j=1}^{3} S_{ij}x_j = D_i, \text{ for } i = 1,2,3.$$

collinearity or spurious causal relationships. However, such indicators are justified on the grounds that the discriminant analysis is for *predictive* purposes; the resultant bias is immaterial as long as predictions are accurate. The danger in following such a rationale is that, even when the underlying economic relationships have changed sufficiently to warrant the revision of the index, management may not have a way of knowing it ahead of time.

To summarize, the discriminant analysis is an excellent filter. However, unless used with precaution, it may prove to be too strong a filter for its economic worth. The decision-tree approach described in the following section provides us with an effective tool to determine when, and where, use of the discriminant analysis would be expedient.

IV. The Decision-Tree Approach

The method proposed here for handling individual requests for credit is known as the "sequential decision process." [8] It rests on two premises. First, because not all relevant information can be secured in time or without cost, not all relevant information is worthwhile in making a decision. Second, past experience can be effectively employed in dealing with uncertainty regarding the future.

The underlying process is simple. Once we acquire a piece of information relevant to the credit-extension decision, we attempt in the light of past experience to estimate the costs associated with the three alternatives: granting credit, rejecting the request, and postponing the decision until some piece of further information is secured. We select that alternative which has the minimum expected cost.

Associated with the granting of credit are the costs of average investment in receivables and of collection efforts made before the final payment. In bad-debt cases, there will be the added cost of the product shipped to the customer. Rejection of a credit request entails loss of the contribution margin composed of profit margin and indirect and overhead cost.[9]

Acceptance cost = (probability of nonpayment) (variable product cost) + average investment cost + average collection cost

Rejection cost = (probability of payment) (contribution margin)

---

[8] For a lucid exposition of this process, see Schlaifer [1959, Chapter 38].

[9] When the volume of sales and production fluctuates widely, the indirect and overhead cost may be replaced by the "unabsorbed" overhead and "indirect burden." Unabsorbed overhead burden is the difference between the burden rate at the "normal" or capacity volume and the standard burden at the actual (or anticipated) volume. As the actual volume approaches the "normal" volume, this difference decreases. Consequently, the rejection cost will be smaller, and the credit standards more stringent, as the actual volume approaches capacity.

Collection cost is based upon the frequency of collection letters, use of stationery and stamps, telegrams (if any), and relevant clerical and supervisory time per credit sale transaction (rather than the volume).

It should be noted here that, as far as the bad-debt cost is concerned, only the variable cost is relevant, because of its incremental nature (fixed cost is a sunk cost).

So far as the investment cost is concerned, normally the variable cost will be relevant. When discounting or factoring the receivables at their face value is undertaken, the sales price would be relevant.[10] Investment cost would also involve the interest-cost component. As was noted in the Introduction to the book, we will utilize the notion of the cost of capital, as suggested in the finance literature, because this concept ensures optimal allocation of resources into various asset forms, including accounts receivable.

The cost of postponing a decision includes two elements: (1) the cost of securing and processing a piece of further information and (2) the *expected* cost of each subsequent move made by chance. This latter element is difficult to explain in the abstract, but it is of crucial importance in the sequential decision process. The difficulty arises because of the use of inductive logic.

The sequential decision process will be explained here by means of an example.

A. Illustration

Suppose a firm relies only on its past experience for evaluating a request for credit. Credit is extended on a net-60-day basis to the approved customers. The firm can make decisions either with or without a review of past experience. The firm classifies its customers into three categories on the basis of past experience: (1) good, (2) poor, and (3) new. The length of the *actual* credit period has been the major criterion for determining these categories:

1. *Good*—Payments have consistently been made within the prescribed period of two months. When the formal credit period has been frequently exceeded, there has been no need for reminders stronger than formal payment reminders or the customer has given a satisfactory explanation for the delinquency.
2. *Poor*—Strong and personal reminders have been necessary in the past, and the amount of credit has, at times, not been reimbursed within a three-month period.
3. *New*—The firm has had no past dealings with the customer requesting credit.

Assume that investigating past records involves $.50 worth of valuable clerical time. Elements of acceptance and rejection costs associated

[10] For a detailed treatment of cost analysis, see Burton [1965, pp. 5–10, 18–21, and 28–36].

with each category of past experience and the alternative of no investigation at all are presented in Table 1–4.

TABLE 1–4

Category of Request	Probability of Payment	Probability of Bad Debt	Average Credit Period	Average Collection Cost
1. No investigation	0.90	0.10	4 months	$0.75
2. Past experience				
Good	1.00	0	2 months	0.25
Poor	0.60	0.40	5 months	4.00
New	0.80	0.20	3 months	1.50

Assume that the sales price is $10 per unit, the contribution margin is $4 per unit, and the cost of capital is 6 percent. When we do not investigate the past experience, and extend the credit immediately to a credit request for X units, the acceptance cost will be the sum of

$$\text{Bad debt cost} + \text{investment cost} + \text{collection cost}$$

$$= (0.10)6X + \left(\frac{0.06}{12}\right)(4 \text{ months})\ (6X) + 0.75$$

$$= 0.6X + 0.12X + 0.75$$

$$= 0.72X + 0.75$$

Similarly, the rejection cost for a request rejected outright will be

$$(0.90)\ (4X)$$

$$= 3.60X$$

Figure 1–1 represents acceptance and rejection costs in the schematic form of a decision tree.

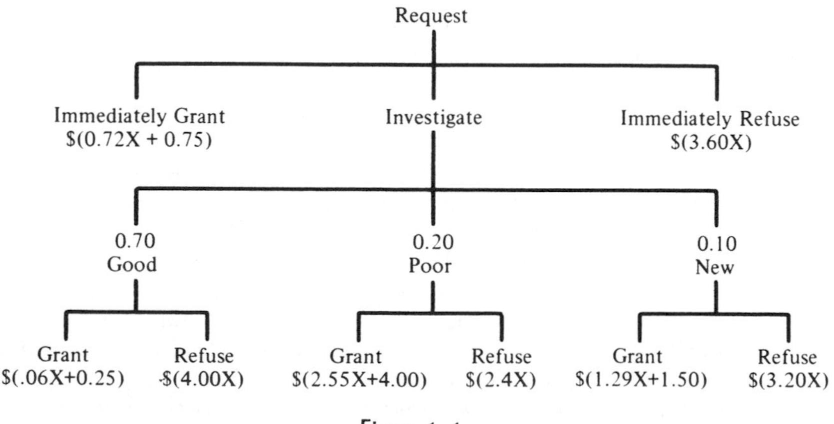

Figure 1–1

When we do not look into past experience at all (i.e., at the first level of the tree) immediate refusal is more expensive than immediate extension of credit. Hence, it is ruled out as an alternative. The "investigate" alternative has a direct cost of $.50; the indirect cost is determined as if we had perfect information about the subsequent decision. If the request falls into either the "good" or "new" category, it will be accepted; if it falls into the "poor" category, it will be rejected. Our past experience indicates that whenever we have investigated our records, 70 percent of the requests have belongd to the "good" category, 20 percent to the "poor" category, and 10 percent to the "new" category.

The *expected* cost of investigation, then, will be

$$\begin{aligned}&\$0.50 \text{ (process cost)}\\&+ (0.70)\ \$(0.25 + 0.06X) + (0.20)\ \$(2.4X) + (0.10)\ \$(1.50 + 1.29X)\\&= \$(0.83 + 0.65X)\end{aligned}$$

Comparing the cost of investigation with the cost of immediate credit extension, we find that immediate credit extension should be given only when a request involves an order for one unit. If the order is larger, the request should be investigated, and it should be refused upon investigation if the record indicates "poor" experience with the account in the past.

B. The Investigation Process

In the example above, there were only two stages of analysis. A typical investigation procedure consists of five stages:

1. No investigation,
2. Past experience,
3. Classification of risk by an outside credit rating agency,
4. References of other creditors and banks,
5. Discriminant analysis of the data in the financial statements.

It should be noted here that there is nothing sacred about the *number* or *order* of these stages. In some companies, for instance, ratings made by an outside agency may not be relied upon; in others, it may be even necessary to conduct a personal interview of the potential customer before making any final decision. In some cases, the order of references and discriminant analysis may be reversed.

The *number* of stages can be increased but, just as in the discriminant analysis, inclusion of a larger number of sources, or more stages, does not necessarily increase the relevant information. Also, an additional stage may entail expenses that immediately rule it out.

The rationale for the *order* of stages listed above is twofold: (1) the process cost of investigation is lower for earlier stages; and (2) inaccessibility of data or delay entailed by this data, increases at later stages. From a slightly different viewpoint, each successive stage may be regarded as a stronger but more expensive filter of requests.

Once the number and order of stages are decided upon, criteria must be devised for dividing each stage into different categories. Generally, management judgment is critical at this juncture.[11]

Cost estimates for each category at various stages enable us to select the least expensive alternative in the same fashion as before. Selection of the optimal alternatives, in turn, provides us with unambiguous rules for routine credit-extension decisions by lower management.

C. Evaluation

The decision-tree approach uses past experience effectively and provides unambiguous operating procedures without jeopardizing the managerial prerogative of formulating policy and making changes in it. However, it does not, by itself, provide an optimal framework. In the first place, improvement stems from past experience, and only in the long run will this approach tend to be optimal. In the second place, the process is static: feedback from implementation of the policy is not incorporated.

V. Control Measures

Both the discriminant analysis and its more generalized version, the decision-tree approach, are based on the premise that past experience is useful for deriving rules for decision making as regards credit extension. However, changes in the relevant conditions, initiated by management or otherwise, decrease the effectiveness of rules that were valid under previous conditions.

An obvious solution is to derive a new set of rules. However, the ability to derive a new set of rules presupposes actual knowledge of changed conditions, which might not be the case. Hence, it is necessary to develop indices, aggregate measures, that flag the attention of management. Even when changes in conditions are deliberately introduced by management, these indices are useful in that they indicate some of the implications of such changes.

Our concern here centers on the financial implications of the decision-making rules: the impact on fund flows of volume of receivables, bad-debt experience, and lost sales.

The task of defining the implications of receivables management as regards fund flows involves the following phases:

1. Identifying variables whose variations set into motion forces that necessitate changes in the decision rules.

---

[11] For a detailed description of devising such criteria, see Mehta [1968].

2. Developing aggregate measures that indicate changes in these variables.
3. Testing the sensitivity of such standards to changes in the variables so as to determine critical variables.

A. Variables Affecting the System

At the outset, we assume that there will be no conscious infringement of rules by lower management which may result in changes in the variables affecting the system. Conscious infringement of rules, of course, is by no means insignificant, but such problems are beyond the scope of this work.

The following are the variables whose behavior will affect the set of decision-making rules:

1. Estimates of uncontrollable[12] costs—cost of capital and product cost.
2. Estimates of controllable and partially controllable costs—process costs of investigation and collection.
3. Length of credit period.
4. Bad-debt experience.
5. Frequency distributions of various *categories* at different *stages* of the investigation process.

Uncontrollable cost estimates are not a direct concern of credit management.

Processing costs of investigation and collection activities are of some significance to credit management. Changes in processing may be at the initiative of credit management. For example, the credit manager may decide to send personal, elaborate, but noncommittal replies to requests that are rejected, instead of impersonal form letters. This procedure may increase the cost of processing. Changes in processing often are not at the initiative of higher management; nor are they meant to be a conscious infringement of the directions of higher management. Fortunately, processing costs are engineering estimates, and deviations are easily revealed by periodic checkups or are reflected in, for example, increased overtime during a given period.

It is the last three categories of variables that are of critical importance to credit management. Credit management is generally evaluated in terms of the average length of credit period (turnover ratio) reflecting the cost of investment in receivables and the bad-debt experience (bad-debt ratio) measuring the bad-debt cost.

Changes in the average credit period and bad-debt experience often affect the frequency distribution of various *categories* at different *stages* of the investigation process. Frequency distributions, in turn, magnify

---

[12] The magnitude of control that can be exercised by management depends on the time element. In the long run investment in fixed assets is controllable. Over a short period of time, such as a day, even wages may be uncontrollable.

or diminish the impact of such changes on relevant costs and associated decision-making rules and fund flows. For instance, various categories of past experience were defined by the criterion of average credit period in our example.

B. Aggregate Indices

Credit-extension decisions, *ceteris paribus,* affect fund flows through the volume of receivables, bad-debt experience, and lost sales. Stringent decisions reduce the volume of receivables and bad debts, but only through increased lost sales. Indiscriminate extension results in decreased lost sales but a larger investment in receivables and an increased bad-debt level.

In our decision-tree example, we used the information provided in Table 1–4 to derive the costs of acceptance and rejection. Thus, the "good" accounts of today may later be reclassified as "poor" because of their tardy payment behavior. On the other hand, bad-debt experience in the "new" category may increase from 20 percent to 30 percent, and in the "poor" category it may decrease from 40 percent to 35 percent. In this case, since 20 percent of the applicants belong to the "poor" category and only 10 percent to the "new" category, the average bad-debt experience may decrease despite a great increase in bad-debt experience in the "new" category.

Let us suppose that in our example the volume of requests for a given month is $10,000, and that no request is for only one unit. Hence, all requests are to be investigated. If the past experience is relevant, data provided in Figure 1–1 and Table 1–4 should enable us to derive the three indices in the form of (1) aging of accounts, (2) lost sales, and (3) bad-debt level.

1. *Aging of accounts.* Figure 1–1 suggests that 70 percent of the requests belong to the "good" category; Table 1–4 indicates that the average credit period of the "good" category is two months. Then, $7,000 worth of receivables should be paid in two months. Similarly, the "new" category will provide us with payments of $1,000 in three months.
2. *Lost sales.* Since requests falling into the "poor" category will be refused, the total amount of rejected requests will be $2,000.
3. *Bad-debt experience.* The probability of bad debt is 0 for the "good" category. This probability is 0.20 for the "new" category. Hence, bad-debt experience will be

$$(.20)(.10)(\$10{,}000) = \$200.$$

Or, we shall write off $200 worth of accounts for every $10,000 in sales requests (or, *actual* credit sales of $8,000).

Although these evaluation measures are similar to the conventional ratio measures criticized earlier, their difference from the conventional measures should be noted. The standards of our measures are logically linked with the set of rules for making routine decisions, rather than determined arbitrarily or in an *ad hoc* fashion.

Whenever the *actual* aging of accounts, lost sales, and bad debts are different from their estimates (derived as noted above) management should be concerned. Of course, the actual values realized for these three indices will rarely correspond exactly to the estimates: it is the extent of deviation that is important. This leads us to the third part of our analysis: testing sensitivity of the three indices to changes in the variables, and distinguishing between random and nonrandom deviations.

C. Sensitivity Analysis

Only an outline of sensitivity analysis will be given here because the procedures underlying such an analysis are similar to those already shown.

Three sets of elements whose estimates will affect the set of decision-making rules, and through these rules the indices, are:

1. Average credit period
2. Probability of default
3. Frequency distribution of different categories at each stage

These estimates are used for measuring the costs of acceptance and rejection as described above. The sensitivity analysis proceeds as follows.

First, upper and lower limits should be established for each element with the help of past experience or managerial judgment.

Second, varying only one subset of elements at a time to their extreme limits (provided by the first step), while keeping all other elements constant, should enable us to derive a set of decision-making rules in the manner indicated in the previous section. If this new set is identical with the set in practice, another subset of variables should be varied for examination—or the third step should be undertaken, if all subsets are exhausted. If the new set is not identical, managerial judgment should be called upon to determine whether the changes in the rules are significant. If they are considered significant, these elements should be first observed when the system is suspected to be out of order. The tolerance limits of these "critical" elements may be established by decreasing their extreme limits initially observed sufficiently to provide a set of rules identical to the present set. This process will provide us with the tolerance limits of the particular subset under observation.

Third, the aggregate indices should be computed for tolerance limits of each subset of elements. This will give us the range of permissible values for the indices. Beyond these ranges, management should regard changes as nonrandom, demanding correction.

Fourth, combinations of various subsets should be made. Their impact on decision rules and indices should be computed. This enables us to determine critical elements and the susceptibility of the system to the changes in such variables. Also, one subset of elements, when combined with another, may have much less impact. In other words, the loss on the one side may be compensated for by the gain on the other. Even though this step appears formidable, it need not be: first, computers can undertake such calculations in a fraction of time; and, second, certain combinations are intuitively more important than others. For instance, in our illustration, "good" past experience comprises 70 percent of the requests. Thus, it is more significant than, say, the "poor" category.

In brief, the simulation process can distinguish "critical" elements through their impact on the set of decision-making rules. At the same time, management can derive the permissible range of receivable volume, bad-debt level, and amount of requests refused through this process. Periodically, then, actual experience can be compared with these indices so as to determine nonrandom fluctations. If fluctuations are nonrandom, reasons for these deviations should be investigated, with particular attention to the subsets of critical elements.

VI. Conclusion

In this chapter, we looked at two analytical approaches dealing with the credit-extension phase of accounts-receivable management. Since credit management exercises its discretion *primarily* during this phase, it is worthwhile to focus attention on this phase. However, the analysis does not ignore the impact of other important aspects of credit management, such as bad-debt levels, length of the credit period, collection activities, and the level of refused requests.

The first analytical approach examined was the discriminant analysis. Its major limitation is that it ignores the economic worth of information. Since credit-extension decisions are critically affected by the investigation process, this limitation is not insignificant. The second approach, the decision-tree method, overcomes this limitation by taking into account the effects of the cost of procuring information. At the same time, it is capable of encompassing the discriminant analysis.

Since decision-making rules derived unambiguously with the help of these approaches are delegated to lower echelons, their effectiveness should be evaluated periodically by management. For this purpose, control measures were suggested in terms of accounts-receivable investment, bad-debt experience, and the amount of requests refused. The strength of these indices lies in their logical relationship to operating decision rules.

The usefulness of the suggested approaches is circumscribed by the following limitations:

1. Collection measures are *decision* variables. Our analysis so far has assumed that collection measures are given. In Chapter 2, we shall focus our attention on this aspect of credit management.
2. Our analytical framework is static. Credit requests from customers are repetitive in nature. Thus, profitability should be measured not only in terms of the current requests but also in terms of expected future requests. Similarly, we need to derive decisions for both the credit-extension phase and collection measures simultaneously. We shall undertake this task in Chapter 3.

2

Collection Measures and Their Effectiveness

I. Introduction

IN Chapter 1 the effects of credit-extension measures on accounts-receivable investment were analyzed. There it was assumed that collection measures and their costs are given. In that case, it is easy to see why changes in collection measures will affect receivables investment. In the decision-tree approach, for instance, we find that a change in the collection cost affects the cost of "acceptance" as well as that of "further investigation"; these costs in turn have an impact on credit-extension decisions and therefore on the receivables investment. This being the case, one possible approach to analyzing the effects of collection measures would be a form of sensitivity analysis within the decision-tree framework. In this chapter, however, we shall discuss an alternative approach that not only is conceptually different from approaches suggested in Chapter 1 but also is useful in integrating two major aspects of credit management—credit-granting decisions and collection measures. For this purpose, we shall reverse the analytical process in this chapter: we shall investigate the effects of changes in collection policy on a receivables level once a credit-granting policy has been established.

Such a partial analysis has conceptual as well as operational relevance. Conceptually, collection measures affect the receivables level directly or indirectly on their own, rather than just through a credit-granting policy. For example, more intensive collection efforts lead directly to larger collections from overdue accounts and thus reduce the receivables investment. Such harsh measures may indirectly affect, in an adverse manner, the firm's goodwill among its customers and thus future business from them. Operationally, our partial analysis would be meaningful for firms where the credit manager has only a nominal control over credit-granting policies, particularly in organizations dominated by the marketing function. In such firms his activity will be confined primarily to determining the intensity with which collection efforts should be pursued for different categories of accounts.

The purpose of this chapter is to evaluate alternatives in collection policy that determine varying intensities of collection efforts before an account is written off.[1] These collection measures affect the *timing* of receipts over several reporting periods and involve periodic expenses once a credit-granting decision is made. Hence, a framework incorporating dynamic cash-flow characteristics is essential for evaluating the effectiveness of alternative collection measures. The conventional capital-budgeting approach seems appropriate for this purpose. However, a direct estimation of relevant cash flows is awkward. As a result, the Markov process is used in this chapter to estimate the relevant cash flows and their discounted value for each of the set of alternatives.

For convenience, we shall ignore here the indirect effects of collection policy in terms of lost goodwill or future sales; however, its impact will be analyzed in the section on integration in Chapter 3, where the interactions between the credit-granting decision and the collection measure will be considered within already-established analytical frameworks.

II. Selection of Collection Policy and Capital Budgeting

A collection policy involves intensity of collection efforts on two dimensions. The first dimension is time. When an account is not paid within the formal credit period, it becomes delinquent. Collection efforts intensify as the period of delinquency increases. Thus, for a "net, 30 days" credit policy, during the first month after the expiration of the credit period, an impersonal, mild reminder may be sent. If it does not produce the desired result, a stronger reminder may be sent during the second month of delinquency. In successive periods of delinquency, still more forceful and harsh measures may be undertaken.

The other dimension is the "quality"of accounts, which is inversely related to their risk potential, reflected in probability of bad debt, ex-

[1] Since no collection efforts are typically made once an account is recognized as a "bad debt," evaluation of collection-policy alternatives also implies determination of the point in time when an account should be written off. Thus our analysis will also determine the optimal length of the credit period or the optimal timing for recognition of a bad debt. Of course, in some firms it is an accepted practice to hand over an account to a collection agency once it reaches a certain "age"; in such firms the account may not be "written off" in the usual sense of the term.

pectation of future business, or both. When these risks are low (i.e., when the quality is high) the collection efforts are mild.

Note that these two dimensions, time and quality, are not totally related. A marginal firm may not take a long time to pay; on the other hand, it is also the experience of some firms that government agencies are extremely slow in their payment habits. Still, we do find that the two dimensions are related in the sense that both attempt to measure risk. In practice, then, both these risk-related dimensions should be considered in determining a collection policy.

Each successive measure of a collection policy may not be completely effective or ineffective, and each may very likely produce partial success. In a given category of accounts, for example, sending the first reminder may produce 50 percent payment on the outstanding amount.

What the above discussion implies is that effects of collection measures are rarely of the nature described by the "point-input, point-output" process. More likely, a series of collection efforts yield a *series* of partial payments. Thus alternative collection policies involve *timing* of cash flows over several reporting periods. This characteristic suggests that evaluation of a collection policy may be possible in the conventional framework of capital budgeting.

An acceptable criterion for selecting a capital-budgeting alternative is maximization of the net present value of cash flows. This proposition raises three related issues:

1. What are the relevant cash flows?
2. How are they measured or estimated?
3. What is the discount rate?

As was noted in the Introduction to the book, the relevant discount rate will be the cost of capital; hence we will not repeat the discussion here.[2]

A. Relevant Cash Flows

The relevant cash flows include collection costs, collection receipts, and bad-debt costs. Collection costs represent costs associated with collection measures; needless to say, these costs are measured in terms of the opportunity cost or incremental cost. For instance, a personal letter to a delinquent account may require some amount of time from the credit manager. Even though he may be a fixed-salary employee, we may figure a proportionate compensation for his time, on the ground that he would have otherwise spent that time on other work.

Collection receipts and bad-debts costs will be defined here as in the previous chapter. Collection receipts will be measured in terms of the contribution margin on the credit amount; bad-debt cost, in terms of incremental, variable cost.

---

[2] Cf. Introduction, p. 4.

B. Cash-flow Estimates

In the conventional approach to capital budgeting, the net present value of a project is derived from discounting net cash flows during its economic life. Where selection of a collection policy is concerned, this procedure immediately raises a problem. What is the economic life of an account? When we deal with *active* accounts, we find that they are often granted credit a second time even before they have paid in full for the first credit extension.

One possibility is to apply the "chain investment" or "replacement" concept prevalent in the literature on capital budgeting.[3] However, this concept is unsatisfactory for our purposes. First, an account's economic life may be constrained either by full payment with no additional requests for credit or by unacceptable delinquency (usually defined by the notion of a "bad debt"). The second constraint is fairly easy to handle, but the first one creates problems. How long should an account remain dormant or inactive if we are not to classify it as an "active" account? A second, closely related, problem is that we are dealing with a large number of active accounts whose economic life may not necessarily be (and usually is not) identical to that of others even in a given risk category. This being the case, how are we to aggregate cash flows, over what period of time? Unless we aggregate cash flows, superiority of one alternative to another is hard to determine. It will be noticed that what we are looking for is a "chain investment" concept that is conditioned in the sense that it provides weights for diverse behavior of accounts in a given category over time.

For this purpose, we may employ the "decision-tree" concept[4] suggested in Chapter 1. However, the approach is clumsy and unwieldy because of the large number of branches (states) involved. For instance, if we write off an account after two months of delinquency for "30 days, net" terms, and even if a category of accounts remains active at most for two months, we will have to consider 53 different alternatives.

Fortunately, a more suitable and expedient approach of estimation is provided by the Markov process; we now turn to a detailed explanation of this method.

* III. The Markov Process and Cash-flow Estimates

To state it very simply, the Markov process enables us to resolve the following issue: If an object moves from one state to another during a period of time, what are the long-run probabilities of that object's being

[3] Cf. Massé [1962, Chapter 2] for elaboration of the concepts of the "chain investment" notion.

[4] For a detailed description of the application along the "decision-tree" approach for capital projects, see Magee [1964].

* Some readers may find the mathematical content of the sections with an asterisk hard to follow. They may skip these sections if they wish.

in each of these states? We shall modify this somewhat for our analysis: If there are "rewards" associated with each of the states, what is the *expected* value of rewards in the long run? Now, cash-flow estimates for an account in a given risk category vary according to the age category of the account and depend upon the planned collection efforts. Thus cash flows are the "rewards," and the age becomes the "state." In order to facilitate the analysis for estimating the cash flows, let us establish a set of relevant definitions.

If the balance of the oldest charge for an account has remained unpaid for i-period, it is defined as "i-period." If an account is written off as a bad debt upon nonpayment in S-period ($S > 1$), i can take the value $0, 1, 2, \ldots, S$.

Suppose that at the *beginning* of a period an account is *current,* i.e., in state 0. Then at the *end* of the period, it is possible for this account to move to only one of the following three states:

1. State A ("fully paid"), when the charge is fully paid
2. 0-state ("current"), when the previous obligation is fully paid, and additional credit is granted within the period under consideration
3. 1-state ("1-period old"), when the previous obligation is not fully paid

Probabilities characterizing these alternatives, respectively, will be p_{0A}, p_{00}, and p_{01}. These probabilities are known as "transition probabilities" for the current state. Note that

$$p_{0i} = 0 \quad \text{for } 1 < i \leq S$$

because it will not be possible for a current account to be, say, 2-period old by the end of one period.

Similarly, we will have transition probabilities for accounts that are 1-period, 2-period, . . . , S-period old at the beginning of a given period. These probabilities, for each of the S periods, as well as states A and $(S + 1)$, are presented in a matrix form, called the "transition matrix," P, below. For convenience, we refer to the $(S + 1)^{\text{th}}$ state as "state B."

$$P = \begin{matrix} p_{AA} & p_{AB} & p_{A0} & \cdots & p_{AS} \\ p_{BA} & p_{BB} & p_{B0} & \cdots & p_{BS} \\ p_{0A} & p_{0B} & p_{00} & \cdots & p_{0S} \\ & & \cdots & & \\ p_{SA} & p_{SB} & p_{S0} & \cdots & p_{SS} \end{matrix}$$

Since each row represents all possible alternatives for transition for a given state, the sum of the elements of each row would be 1. Now an account that is fully paid cannot move to any other state; similarly, a bad-debt account will not be extended any additional credit. Hence,

$$p_{AA} = p_{BB} = 1$$

$$p_{Ai} = p_{Bj} = 0 \quad \text{for } i \neq A \text{ and } j \neq B$$

Thus, the transition matrix P can be written as

$$P = \left[\begin{array}{cc|ccc} 1 & 0 & 0 & \cdots & 0 \\ 0 & 1 & 0 & \cdots & 0 \\ \hline r_{0A} & r_{0B} & q_{00} & \cdots & q_{0S} \\ & & \cdots & & \\ r_{SA} & r_{SB} & q_{S0} & & q_{SS} \end{array}\right]$$

where $r_{iA} = p_{iA}$, $r_{iB} = p_{iB}$, and $q_{ij} = p_{ij}$ for $i, j = 0, 1, \ldots, S$

Then we may characterize the P matrix as

$$P = \left[\begin{array}{c|c} I & 0 \\ \hline R & Q \end{array}\right]$$

where I is an identity matrix and 0 is a null matrix.

The partitioned matrix Q is square, and it represents all nonabsorbing states, i.e., states from which it is possible to move out (only A and B are absorbing states).

Let α, β, . . . designate the policy alternatives under consideration. Our problem is to determine net cash flows associated with each of these policy alternatives for a predetermined number of periods, say, t ($t > 1$). Let $L_i\ (t,\alpha)$ represent the sum of undiscounted net receipts over t periods from an account that is initially i-period old under the policy alternative α. Then, $L_i\ (t,\alpha)$ will be given by three components:

1. Average receipts from accounts that are absorbed in the coming period (either in A or B)
2. Receipts in the coming period that accrue because of transition to any of the nonabsorbing states, j, plus the net receipts in the subsequent ($t - 1$) periods for accounts that are j-period old
3. Collection expenditure, $F_{i\alpha}$, on an i-period-old account in the coming period (note that $F_{i\alpha}$ will be a decision variable).

Let c_{ij} represent the receipt from an i-period-old account that will be in state j at the end of one period for all nonabsorbing states. Note that c_{ij} represents the face value of corresponding receivables and not their contribution margin, and that it is not adjusted for cash outlays for collection. Then c_{iA} (positive) represents the receipt from the account that is fully paid; and c_{iB} (negative) represents the face value of the account that is written off. We thus have a collection (receipt) matrix, C.[5] For the incremental, variable cost per dollar of sales, d, we get

$$L_i(t,\alpha) = (1 - d)r_{iA}c_{iA} + dr_{iB}c_{iB} + \sum_{j=0}^{S} q_{ij}[(1 - d)c_{ij} + L_j(t - 1)] - F_{i\alpha}, \tag{1}$$

$$\text{for } i = 0, 1, \ldots, S$$

From this recursive relationship, as is shown in Appendix A, we get undiscounted net receipts from an i-period-old account under alternative α by

$$L_i(\alpha) = \sum_{j=0}^{S} n_{ij}[(1 - d)p_{jA}c_{jA} + dp_{jB}c_{jB} + \sum_{k=0}^{S} (1 - d)p_{jk}c_{jk} - F_{j\alpha}], \tag{2}$$

where $[n_{ij}] = N = (I - Q)^{-1}$ for $i, j = 0, 1, \ldots, S$

and I is an identity matrix.

The element n_{ij} represents the average number of times an i-period-old account will be in state j before it is ultimately absorbed in state A or B. $[(1 - d)p_{jA}c_{jA}]$ represents the conditional contribution from absorption in state A for a j-period-old account; $[dp_{jB}c_{jB}]$ is the incremental bad-debt cost; and $[(1 - d)p_{jk}c_{jk}]$ gives us the net conditional receipts from transition to all nonabsorbing states k. Thus the expression on the right side of equation (2) represents the product of the number of times an i-period-old account will make transition to the jth state and the conditional net receipts from state j, where i and j represent all nonabsorbing states.

If x_i is the initial number of accounts that are i-period old, the product

$$x_i L_i(\alpha)$$

gives us the total receipts from all i-period-old accounts. The quantity

$$\sum_{i=0}^{S} x_i L_i(\alpha) \tag{3}$$

gives us the conditional expected net receipts for a policy alternative.

The value $DL_i(\alpha)$, representing $L_i(\alpha)$ discounted at the rate of e, is given by (as shown in Appendix A):

---

[5] The collection matrix, C, is similar to Howard's notion of the reward matrix [1960]. His formulation of the problem requires selection of the *optimal* alternative i as a starting point that maximizes the reward. In our case, the starting point is always 0, the current state. Hence his mode of solution based on the Z-transformation (or the Laplace transform for continuous probability distributions) is not required for our purpose.

$$DL_i(\alpha) = \sum_{j=0}^{S} n_{vij}[(1-d)p_{jA}c_{jA} + dp_{jB}c_{jB} + \sum_{k=0}^{S}(1-d)p_{jk}c_{jk} - F_{j\alpha}] \quad (4)$$

where $$[n_{vij}] = N_v = (I - VQ)^{-1}$$

and $$V = \frac{1}{1+e}$$

The sum $$\sum_{i=0}^{S} x_i DL_i(\alpha) \quad (5)$$

will give us the present value of net receipts from all accounts under collection-policy alternative α. When we have a number of collection-policy alternatives, we will find this value for each alternative, and select whichever policy alternative has the largest present value.

So far we have not resolved the issue of the lost-sales cost connected with stringent collection measures. This lost-sales cost is often too insignificant to be considered.[6] Even when it is significant, it is not, here, amenable to being estimated in a systematic, objective fashion. In this case, the manager may rely on his own judgment (or on that of the marketing department) in formulating cost estimates.

The advantage of the proposed method is that it enables us to estimate both transient *and* steady-state cash flows after *one* credit-extension period.[7] The reliability of these estimates can be readily ascertained with the help of equation (1) because that relationship directly provides us with the desired estimates for the second period, third period, and so on. However, in order to make flows comparable with these estimates, we have to adjust the actual flows for their economic worth; i.e., only contribution margins on collection receipts and incremental, variable costs for bad-debt and collection expenditures would be relevant for purposes of comparison.

Since our estimates are *point* estimates, it may be desirable at times to have appropriate *ranges* for them. When this is the case, one may first compute *variances* of estimates, as suggested by Cyert, Davidson, and Thompson [1962, pp. 296–297]; then one may establish appropriate

[6] Insignificant lost-sales cost implies that we can take for granted the sales level for our analysis. Note, however, that for *credit-granting* purposes, this cost would be significant. To this extent our model needs modification before it can be applied to the selection of credit-granting decisions. In Chapter 3, a procedure is suggested to estimate lost-sales cost from refused requests in a framework of integrated credit policy.

[7] As is shown in Appendix B, Beranek's proposal [1963], an extension of Cyert, Davidson, and Thompson's work [1962], for selecting an efficient alternative ignores cash flows *prior* to the point of equilibrium (steady state). It should be noted that the primary purpose of Cyert, Davidson, and Thompson's work is estimating relevant credit information for *reporting* purposes, and they only indicated the *potential* of their model for *selection* of credit policy (pp. 299–300).

confidence limits,[8] which, in turn, would provide the confidence interval or range. If the estimates are reliable, then actual outcomes will fall within this range. If they fall outside the range, the estimates are unreliable, and one must take corrective measures, such as using another sample or a larger sample.

IV. Application

The following simple illustration demonstrates the applicability of the proposed model and pinpoints the need for relevant data.

The firm under observation sells a product on "30 days, net" credit terms. Field salesmen are authorized to grant credit to a customer up to $500 per month, unless his account is on a special list, which indicates that collection experience in the past has been too poor to warrant any further extension of credit. Primarily, accounts on this list are bad debts that have been written off because they were not collected within three months of the granting of credit (or two months after the contractual credit period was over).

At present, the credit manager has two alternatives with respect to collection expense per account.

Collection Expense per Account

	Existing Situation	Proposed Alternative
Current	$10	$ 5
1 month overdue	$20	$10
2 months overdue	$25	$30

The proposed alternative represents less stringent collection measures in the first two months, to be followed by more intensive efforts in the third month.

For every ten accounts, four accounts are current, four are one month overdue, and two are two months overdue.

The contribution margin on the product is $0.33 per dollar of sales. Credit sales do not have any seasonal or cyclical pattern.

Credit files are arranged alphabetically for each of three geographical regions. On March 1, 1970, the credit manager selected seventy requests from each region and divided them into two groups. The proposed alternative was to be applied to one group during the month of March; for the second group, the current practice was to be continued.

[8] In some cases, it is likely that the initial "spillover" effects from the existing policy cause excessive variability of estimates. If we are to assume that these effects will wear out over time, then it may be necessary to apply variable confidence limits for successive periods. For instance, one may employ a 99 percent confidence interval for the second and third periods, and 95 percent intervals thereafter.

On March 31, 1970, the credit manager prepared for each alternative the following tables, which classified accounts according to age and commensurate average payments. From these data, he prepared a frequency distribution for each cell. For instance, forty accounts were current on March 1, and fifteen of them were fully paid under the existing situation. Hence, p_{0A} is 15/40, or 3/8. Similarly, 15 initially current accounts that became one month old on March 31 released partial receipts worth $900. Hence, c_{01} is 900/15, or $60.

A. The Existing Situation

March 1 \ March 31	Fully Paid	Current	1 Month Overdue	2 Months Overdue	Bad Debt	Total
Current	15	10	15	0	0	40
1 month overdue	12	9	9	15	0	45
2 months overdue	3	4	4	6	3	20

Transition Matrix

$$P(A) = \left[\begin{array}{cc|ccc} A & B & 0 & 1 & 2 \\ 1 & 0 & 0 & 0 & 0 \\ 0 & 1 & 0 & 0 & 0 \\ \hline \frac{3}{8} & 0 & \frac{1}{4} & \frac{3}{8} & 0 \\ \frac{1}{5} & 0 & \frac{1}{5} & \frac{4}{15} & \frac{1}{3} \\ \frac{3}{20} & \frac{3}{20} & \frac{1}{5} & \frac{1}{5} & \frac{3}{10} \end{array}\right]$$

Collection Per Account *Collection Expense*

$$C(A) = \begin{array}{ccccc} A & B & 0 & 1 & 2 \\ 0 & 0 & 0 & 0 & 0 \\ 0 & 0 & 0 & 0 & 0 \\ 150 & (150) & 150 & 60 & 0 \\ 225 & (225) & 225 & 115 & 75 \\ 270 & (270) & 270 & 75 & 75 \end{array} \qquad F(A) = \begin{array}{c} 10 \\ 20 \\ 25 \end{array}$$

B. The Proposed Alternative

March 1 \ March 31	Fully Paid	Current	1 Month Overdue	2 Months Overdue	Bad Debt	Total
Current	10	10	10	0	0	30
1 month overdue	11	11	11	22	0	55
2 months overdue	5	2	6	5	2	20

Transition Matrix

$$P(B) = \begin{array}{cc|ccc} A & B & 0 & 1 & 2 \\ 1 & 0 & 0 & 0 & 0 \\ 0 & 1 & 0 & 0 & 0 \\ \hline \frac{1}{3} & 0 & \frac{1}{3} & \frac{1}{3} & 0 \\ \frac{1}{5} & 0 & \frac{1}{5} & \frac{1}{5} & \frac{2}{5} \\ \frac{1}{4} & \frac{1}{10} & \frac{1}{10} & \frac{3}{10} & \frac{1}{4} \end{array}$$

Collection Matrix *Collection Expense*

$$C(B) = \begin{array}{ccccc} A & B & 0 & 1 & 2 \\ 0 & 0 & 0 & 0 & 0 \\ 0 & 0 & 0 & 0 & 0 \\ 143 & (143) & 143 & 55 & 0 \\ 231 & (231) & 231 & 100 & 60 \\ 275 & (275) & 275 & 110 & 132 \end{array} \qquad F(B) = \begin{array}{c} \\ \\ 5 \\ 10 \\ 30 \end{array}$$

For $V = \dfrac{1}{1.02}$, and $d = \dfrac{2}{3}$,

$$N_v(A) = (I - VQ_A)^{-1} = \begin{array}{ccc} 0 & 1 & 2 \\ 1.64 & .84 & .39 \\ .53 & 1.60 & .45 \\ .64 & .71 & 1.74 \end{array}$$

and

$$N_v(B) = (I - VQ_B)^{-1} = \begin{array}{ccc} 0 & 1 & 2 \\ 1.81 & .90 & .47 \\ .63 & 1.88 & .97 \\ .50 & .85 & 1.76 \end{array}$$

	Alternative A	Alternative B
DL_0	\$70.07	\$93.49
DL_1	\$61.24	\$94.76
DL_2	\$26.49	\$56.85

On March 1, there were 1,000 accounts current; 1,000 accounts one month overdue; and 500 accounts two months overdue. Hence, the net collections under the proposed alternative will be \$216,675—as against \$144,555 under the existing policy. If the cost estimate for incremental lost good will for the proposed alternatives does not exceed \$72,120,[9] the proposed alternative should be accepted.

V. Conclusion

The intensity of collection efforts and the length of the credit period are areas where alternatives are available to management. However, even when the alternatives are clearly defined, their individual implications for cash-flow behavior are complex and dynamic. In this chapter, we have examined an expedient method, based on the Markov process, for selecting the most efficient of the available collection-policy alternatives. The suggested model focuses on the timing and behavior of cash flows during transition[10] as well as in the state of equilibrium (steady state). It revises probabilities contingent upon the age (state) of an account, and it explicitly accounts for alternative collection costs and efforts.

The strength of the model is its modest inputs of data: it requires only the initial number of accounts in each age category, the transition probability, and receipts from transition during one credit period

[9] Reduction of collection expenses during earlier periods will probably indicate that the *incremental* lost-sales cost for the proposed alternative is negative.

[10] We may look at the significance of the transient component with the help of an analogy. In capital budgeting processes, the payback method is criticized for ignoring the useful life of, and related cash flows from, an alternative *after* a predetermined point. This does not mean that we may not select an optimal capital-expenditure alternative. It would, however, be difficult to guarantee that we will *always* select the optimal course of action. Similarly, Beranek's suggestion, which ignores cash flows from a short-lived asset with relatively high turnover *before* the equilibrium point, cannot assure us selection of the optimal collection-cost strategy.

(month). Moreover, it extrapolates future stochastic cash-flow behavior with relative simplicity.

The model facilitates the integration of credit extension and formulation of collection policy, which is taken up in Chapter 3.

Appendix A

$$\text{Let } [p_{ij}] = P, \text{ the probability matrix } = \frac{I \mid 0}{R \mid Q}$$

for $\quad i, j = A, B, 0, 1, \ldots, S$

where Q is a square matrix and I is a square identity matrix

$[c_{ij}] = C$, the payment matrix corresponding to P

$d =$ incremental cost per dollar of sales

$[m_{ij}] = [kp_{ij}c_{ij}] = M$, the conditional average payment matrix

where $k = (1 - d)$ for $j = A, 0, 1, \ldots, S$; $k = d$ for $j = B$

$e =$ the discount rate

$V = (1 + e)^{-1}$

$[n_{ij}] = N = (I - Q)^{-1}$

$[n_{vij}] = N_v = (I - VQ)^{-1}$

$L_i(t,\alpha) =$ net undiscounted receipts from i-period-old accounts in the forthcoming t-periods. α indicates the related collection-policy alternative. (We will henceforth omit α unless necessary.)

$DL_i(t) =$ discounted net receipts from i-period-old accounts

$\lambda =$ a vector containing $(S + 2)$ elements each having value 1.

Then, equation (1) gives

$$L_i(t) = (1 - d)p_{iA}c_{iA} + dp_{iB}c_{iB} + \sum_{j=0}^{S} (1 - d)q_{ij}c_{ij} - F_i$$
$$+ \sum_{j=0}^{S} q_{ij}L_j(t - 1), \quad \text{for } i = 0, 1, \ldots, S \tag{A-1}$$
$$= m_{iA} + m_{iB} + \sum_{j=0}^{S} m_{ij} + \sum_{j=0}^{S} q_{ij}L_j(t - 1) - F_i$$

In matrix notation,

$$\begin{aligned} L(t) &= M\lambda + QL(t-1) \\ &= M\lambda + Q[M\lambda + QL(t-2)] \\ &= M\lambda + QM\lambda + Q^2L(t-2) \\ &= M\lambda + QM\lambda + Q^2M\lambda + \cdots + Q^{t-1}M\lambda + Q^tL(0). \end{aligned}$$

Since $L(0) = 0,$

$$L(t) = (I + Q + Q^2 + \cdots + Q^{t-1})M\lambda$$

and since $\underset{t\to\infty}{Lt}\, Q^t = 0$, for a sufficiently large value of t,

we get

$$\begin{aligned} L &= (I - Q)^{-1}M\lambda \\ &= NM\lambda, \quad \text{or} \end{aligned}$$

$$L_i = \sum_{j=0}^{S} n_{ij}[m_{jA} + m_{jB} - F_j + \sum_{j=0}^{S} m_{jk}] \tag{A-2}$$

When we apply the discount factor to (A-1), we get

$$DL_i = (1-d)r_{iA}c_{iA} + dr_{iB}c_{iB} - F_i + (1-d)\sum_{j=0}^{S} q_{ij}c_{ij} + V\sum_{j=0}^{S} q_{ij}L_j(t-1) \tag{A-3}$$

Hence,

$$\begin{aligned} DL(t) &= M\lambda + VQL(t-1) \\ &= M\lambda + VQ[M\lambda + VQL(t-2)] \\ &= M\lambda + VQM\lambda + V^2Q^2L(t-2) \end{aligned}$$

Then,

$$\begin{aligned} DL &= (I - VQ)^{-1}M\lambda \\ &= N_vM\lambda, \quad \text{or} \end{aligned}$$

$$DL_i = \sum_{j=0}^{S} n_{vij}[(1-d)r_{jA}c_{jA} + dr_{jB}c_{jB} - F_j + (1-d)\sum_{k=0}^{S} r_{jk}c_{jk}] \tag{A-4}$$

Appendix B

Beranek [1963, Chapter 10] suggests that the model of Cyert, Davidson, and Thompson [1962] should be modified in the following way. We should select the policy alternative that maximizes

$$\sum_{i=0}^{S} \sum_{j=0}^{S} y_i n_{ij}[(1-d)r_{jA} - dr_{jB}],^1 \qquad \text{(B-1)}$$

where y_i is the aging of i-period-old accounts.

In this format, equation (B-1) is similar to equation (3), with one exception: equation (B-1) deals with cash flow per period, whereas equation (3) encompasses cash flows for t periods. If we divide (3) by t, both forms will be compatible for purposes of comparison. Thus,

$$\text{(B-1)} = \frac{1}{t} \text{ equation (3)}$$

if:
$$t \sum_{i=0}^{S} \sum_{j=0}^{S} y_i n_{ij}[(1-d)r_{jA} - dr_{jB}] = \sum_{i=0}^{S} x_i L_i(t)$$

or:
$$\sum_{i=0}^{S} \sum_{j=0}^{S} y_i n_{ij}[(1-d)r_{jA} - dr_{jB}] = \frac{1}{t} \sum_{i=0}^{S} \sum_{j=0}^{S} x_i n_{ij}[(1-d)c_{jA}r_{jA} + dc_{jB}r_{jB} + (1-d) \sum_{k=0}^{S} q_{jk}c_{jk}].$$

Since
$$c_{iA} = -c_{iB}$$

and
$$y_i = x_i c_{iA} = -x_i c_{iB}$$

the equality will hold, if

$$\sum_{i=0}^{S} \sum_{j=0}^{S} x_i c_{iA} n_{ij}[(1-d)r_{jA} - dr_{jB}] - \frac{1}{t} \sum_{i=0}^{S} \sum_{j=0}^{S} x_i c_A n_{ij}[(1-d)r_{jA} - dr_{jB}] = \frac{1}{t}(1-d) \sum_{i=0}^{S} \sum_{j=0}^{S} \sum_{k=0}^{S} x_i n_{ij} q_{jk} c_{jk}$$

Or,

$$\sum_{i=0}^{S} \sum_{j=0}^{S} x_i c_{iA} n_{ij}[(1-d)r_{jA} - dr_{jB}](c_{iA} - c_{jA}/t) = \sum_{i=0}^{S} \sum_{j=0}^{S} \sum_{k=0}^{S} x_i n_{ij} q_{jk} c_{jk} \qquad \text{(B-2)}$$

---

[1] Beranek does not adjust cash inflows, r_{jA}, by $(1-d)$ [1963, pp. 319–20]; for purposes of comparison, this adjustment is made here.

$q_{jk} \geq 0$ because it represents the transition probabilities. Collections would be negative only when an account is written off; and an account is written off only at the end of Sth period. Hence

$$r_{jB} = 0, \quad \text{for } j < S, \quad \text{and}$$

$$c_{jk} \geq 0, \quad \text{for } j, k = 1, 2, \ldots, S$$

The quantity $q_{jk}c_{jk}$ on the right side of equation (B-2) will be non-negative for any particular value of j, $k \leq S$. Moreover, $q_{jk}c_{jk}$ will be zero only if a live account does not pay anything until it is absorbed in either state A or state B. A current account, for example, would either be paid in full or be 1-period old, but it would not remain current (by paying the current debt and incurring an additional charge during the same period); or, in general, an account would never make a part payment on the outstanding amount.

Under a more likely situation, however, $q_{jk}c_{jk}$ will be positive at least for some values of j, $k \leq S$. Then at least some terms on the right side of equation (B-2) will be positive. For the term-by-term comparison of two sides, the left side of equation (B-2) will not be positive, when

1. For $j < S$, $c_{iA} \leq c_{jA}/t$
2. For $j = S$, $r_{jA} \leq dr_{jB}$ and $c_{iA} \geq c_{jA}/t$, or
   $r_{jA} \geq dr_{jB}$ and $c_{iA} \leq c_{jA}/t$

Then *at least* under these circumstances,[2] the equality will not be maintained, and the Beranek model (left side) will understate the cash flows. A simple example illustrates this point.

Let $P(1)$, $P(2)$ represent transition matrices for two alternative credit policies:

$$P(1) = \begin{matrix} 1 & 0 & 0 \\ 0 & 1 & 0 \\ .4 & .1 & .5 \end{matrix} \quad P(2) = \begin{matrix} 1 & 0 & 0 \\ 0 & 1 & 0 \\ .2 & .05 & .75 \end{matrix} \quad C(1) = C(2) = \begin{matrix} 0 & 0 & 0 \\ 0 & 0 & 0 \\ 100 & (100) & 100 \end{matrix}$$

$$d = .5 \qquad Y(1) = Y(2) = \$100 \qquad x = 1$$

$$N(1) = 2 \qquad N(2) = 4$$

[2] Even when both sides are positive, there is no guarantee that

$$(r_{jA} - dr_{jB})(c_{iA} - \underline{c_{jA}}) = \frac{1}{t} q_{jk}c_{jk},$$

hence the qualification.

According to Beranek's approach [equation (B-1)],

$$XNR(1) = 100 \times 2[.2 - .05] \qquad XNR(2) = 100 \times 4[.1 - .025]$$
$$= \$40 - \$10 \qquad\qquad = \$40 - \$10$$
$$= \$30 \qquad\qquad = \$30$$

The proposed approach will give us:

$$L(1) = \$2(20 - 5 + 25) \qquad L(2) = \$4(10 - 2.50 + 37.50)$$
$$= \$(90 - 10) = \$80 \qquad\qquad = \$(190 - 10) = \$180$$

Hence we should select the second policy alternative. This seems reasonable because a current account will remain current for a longer time under the second alternative, and would thereby reduce the magnitude of credit loss *per period.* The calculations above show that the bad-debt component ($10) remains the same under both approaches. However, the pattern of payment differs. Under the first alternative, the system achieves stability after the *first* period; under the second alternative, it achieves stability after the *third* period. Beranek's approach takes into account net cash inflows only when the system achieves stability ($40). The proposed approach shows net cash inflows of $50 for the first period (before stability) and $40 for the second period under the first alternative. Similarly, under the second alternative, inflows would be $50 for each of the first three periods and $40 for the fourth period. Hence, the net receipt *per period* will be $40 for the first alternative and $45 for the second alternative.

Thus Beranek's approach will understate total (or average) collections and to that extent will overstate bad-debt estimates. The larger the number of periods during which the system remains dynamic, the larger the discrepancy between the estimates of the two approaches we have discussed. This discrepancy would be, needless to say, immaterial (while comparing two alternatives) only when the behavior of the transient components (in the above example, $10) is consistent with the steady-state values in such a way that inclusion or exclusion of the transient components would not reverse the selection of an alternative. *A priori* justification of the idea that such a discrepancy is immaterial is not possible.

Credit Policy Integration

I. Introduction

In the previous two chapters, attention was focused on two major facets of credit management:

1. rules for making credit-granting decisions;
2. selection of a collection policy.

The basic weakness of the approaches suggested was that the analysis of each aspect assumed exogenous determination of the other. As we have seen, these two decision variables are closely interrelated and thus should be determined simultaneously. In this chapter, the decision-tree approach for credit granting will be related to the Markov process to formulate an optimal integrated credit policy.

This integration enables us to overcome other shortcomings also, particularly shortcomings of the decision-tree approach. First, forces affecting the estimates for acceptance or rejection costs were to be observed over the period covering the execution of an order and its normal recognition as a bad debt. Furthermore, reliable estimates of bad-debt costs and investment costs may not be possible *before* the underlying dynamic forces have achieved equilibrium, but this may entail an excessively long waiting period. For example, suppose that a firm recognizes an account as a bad debt when it remains unpaid for six months after credit has been granted. If the firm wants to determine the effects of a credit-policy alternative on bad-debt experience, the manager has to determine a suitable time period (say, eight months) at the end of which he would have reliable information on bad-debt cost. If the period is shorter than that, he faces a danger of possibly unstable cost estimates; at the same time, he may find that the "suitable period" is too long a time to postpone a decision or an alternative course of action. Second, control indices that reflect details of operating decision rules would also not be expediently (and reliably) determined in a reasonable time period. Thus, in the above example it would take at least six months to devise the set of control indices.

For this purpose, the Markov process will be utilized to derive necessary cost estimates for the decision-making rules to be applied to individual requests; then, when a stable set of decision-making rules is devised through an iterative process for each of the alternative credit policies, selection of the optimal alternatives will be made; finally, a procedure for deriving relevant control indices for the optimal alternative will be suggested.

Conceptual refinements underlying this attempt naturally lead to apparently complex, if not cumbersome, formulae. However, the reiterative computation procedure is amenable to computer programming; moreover, as the illustration shows, the input requirements are surprisingly modest.

II. Cost Estimates

When a request for credit arrives, we determine the costs of accepting and rejecting it and then decide whether the request should be granted. As was noted in Chapter 1, the acceptance cost for each level of information is determined by factors such as the probability of payment (or nonpayment), the size of the current request, the outstanding balance (if any), and the estimated length of the credit period. Similarly, the rejection cost involves the realizable contribution margin on the current request only. Now the Markov process can be directly applied to the acceptance-cost estimate; moreover, the same line of reasoning can be applied to the rejection or lost-sales cost that incorporates the realizable margin on the current request as well as future business in the wake of it.

* A. Acceptance Cost

If an account with the outstanding amount x_i is initially i-period old, p_{ij} is the probability that it will be j-period old at the end of the period, where $j \leq i + 1$. To be consistent with the previous chapter, let us define *current* accounts as 0-period old; accounts that are *fully paid* without any additional credit request during the period as belonging to the A state; and accounts that are *credit losses* as belonging to the B state. Thus we have a transition probability matrix $[p_{ij}]$, where

$$1 \geq p_{ij} \geq 0, \qquad \text{for } i, j = A, B, 0, 1, \ldots, S$$

and $S =$ the length of effective credit period.

Associated with $[p_{ij}]$, is the payment matrix $[c_{ij}]$, where c_{ij} is the payment received from an account initially i-period old, but j-period old at the end of one period. It should be noted that c_{iB} would be the negative amount of the outstanding account that is written off as a bad debt.

Now $[p_{ij}]$ can be partitioned (see Chapter 2) as follows:

$$[p_{ij}] = \begin{array}{c|c} I & 0 \\ \hline R & Q \end{array}$$

where $I =$ identity matrix $(i = 2, j = 2)$

$0 =$ null matrix $(i = 2, j = S - 2)$

R, Q are matrices with $(i = S - 2, j = 2)$ and $(i = S - 2, j = S - 2)$ respectively

Let F_i be the amount of collection expenditure spent on an account i-period old. If $e =$ the discount rate, $V = \dfrac{1}{(1 + e)}$ is the discounted value of the payment received one period from now. d is the ratio of incremental cost to the sales price of the product. If an account is i-period old now, $DL_i(T)$, the discounted value of incremental cash inflow in T periods, will be given by:

1. Incremental receipts in the first period that accrue from transition to the j-period-old category, *plus* the discounted net (incremental) receipts in the subsequent $(T - 1)$ periods for accounts that will be j-period old, for $j = 0, 1, \ldots, S$ *times* the transition probability, p_{ij}
2. Expected value of net receipts from absorption states A and B
3. Collection expense

Thus,

$$DL_i(T) = (1 - d)p_{iA}c_{iA} + dp_{iB}c_{iB} - F_i + \sum_{j=0}^{S} p_{ij}[(1 - d)c_{ij} + DL_j(T - 1)] \qquad (1)$$

As was noted in Chapter 2, this leads to

$$DL_i(T) = \sum_{j=0}^{S} n_{vij}[(1-d)p_{jA}c_{jA} + dp_{jB}c_{jB} + \sum_{k=0}^{S}(1-d)p_{jk}c_{jk} - F_j] \quad (2)$$

where $[n_{vij}] = (I - VQ)^{-1}$

Acceptance cost for an i-period-old account, $AC_i(T)$, involves the sum of the investment cost, the discounted incremental bad-debt cost, and the discounted collection cost. Bad-debt cost is an extension of investment cost on the time scale. Hence, if we take the difference between the time-adjusted incremental value of orders and discounted probabilistic inflows related to incremental cost, it will give us the sum of desired bad-debt and investment costs.[1]

Hence,

$AC_i(T)$ = discounted value of orders − discounted incremental probabilistic *in*flows + discounted collection cost

= discounted value of orders − (discounted incremental probabilistic inflows − discounted collection cost)

Comparison between the expression in the parentheses and $DL_i(T)$ indicates that $DL_i(T)$ includes probabilistic inflows in terms of contribution margin rather than incremental cost, and that there is a separate term for discounted net bad-debt costs. We will get the required parenthetical expression if we modify $DL_i(T)$ by:

1. Multiplying c_{jA} and c_{jk} by d instead of $(1 - d)$
2. Removing the term containing c_{jB}

---

[1] By direct reasoning, bad-debt cost + investment cost = (incremental order cost) (probability of nonpayment) (discount factor) + (incremental order cost) (1 − discount factor)

Thus, if incremental order cost = \$90, discount factor = .8, p_{iB} = .3.

Bad-debt cost + investment cost = (90)(.3)(.8) + (90)(.2)
= 21.60 + 18 = \$39.60

Time-adjusted incremental order value − discounted incremental probabilistic inflow = (90) − (.8)(90)(.7) = 90 − 50.40 = \$39.60

The advantage of the indirect definition is obvious: when we consider multiperiod flows, an adaption of the Markov-process estimates simplifies the calculation of acceptance cost.

It should be noted that both order value and inflows are stated in terms of incremental product cost. thus netting the contribution margin.

Thus:

$$\begin{aligned} AC_i(T) &= \text{discounted incremental value of orders} \\ &\quad - \text{modified } DL_i(T) \\ &= \text{discounted incremental value of orders} \\ &\quad - \sum_{j=0}^{S} n_{vij}[dp_{jA}c_{jA} + d\sum_{k=0}^{S} p_{jk}c_{jk} - F_j] \end{aligned} \quad (3)$$

In order to maintain consistency between the discounted value of orders and the size of the orders implied by the modified value of $_{DLi}(T)$, we should take into account not only the current credit request, O_{ij}, but also the outstanding balance, x_i, adjusted for discount rate, *and* the discounted value of future orders. Here we rule out three alternative ways of measuring the size of the order: (1) the current credit request alone; (2) outstanding balance *plus* current credit request; and (3) current credit request *plus* future credit requests. Alternative 1 would have been acceptable, had we made the assumption that the cost of past extension(s) is a sunk cost, and thereby is irrelevant, and the corollary assumption that future decisions will not be affected by the current decision. Practical experience of credit executives indicates that a customer's ability to pay is affected by the size of the outstanding balance; thus approval of the current credit request may affect (and be affected by) the size of the outstanding balance. Moreover, approval of the current credit request may imply involuntary future extensions. If we do not assume that the present decision is independent of past actions or the future, alternatives 2 and 3 will also be unacceptable.

A legitimate objection to the recommended alternative is: If we are already taking future requests into account, why should we investigate an account each time a request comes in? And if this is so, should we not investigate for the credit-extension limit only if there is no outstanding balance at all?

It should be noted that the decision rules derived will indicate not only whether to extend credit but also, presumably, to what extent; thus computation of costs will not be necessary each time a request comes in, particularly when it is from a customer having an active account. On the other hand, decision rules should take into account interrelated actions; otherwise, they will lead to nonoptimal decisions.

The current outstanding balance, x_i, includes variable cost, overhead cost, and profit margin. If d is the ratio of variable cost to sales price, the present value of the outstanding balance will be $dx_i(1 + e)^i$ [2]

The value of current and future requests, $dVF_i(T)$, is given by

---

[2] For convenience, it is assumed that the outstanding balance, x_i has resulted from one (rather than more than one) credit order in the past.

$$VF_i(T) = \sum_{j=0}^{S} p_{ij}[O_{ij} + V \cdot VF_j(T-1)]$$
$$= \sum_{j=0}^{S} q_{ij}O_{ij} + V \sum_{j=0}^{S} q_{ij}VF_j(T-1)$$
$$= \overline{O}_i + V \sum_{j=0}^{S} q_{ij}VF_j(T-1)$$

In matrix notation,

$$VF(T) = \overline{O} + V \cdot Q \cdot VF(T-1)$$
$$= \overline{O} + V \cdot Q[\overline{O} + VQVF(T-2)]$$
$$= \overline{O} + V \cdot Q\overline{O} + (VQ)^2 VF(T-2)$$

as in equation (1),

$$VF(T) = (1 - VQ)^{-1}\overline{O}$$
$$= N_v\overline{O}, \quad \text{or}$$
$$dVF_i(T) = d \sum_{j=0}^{S} n_{vij} \left[\sum_{k=0}^{S} q_{jk}O_{jk} \right] \tag{4}$$

If X is the actual amount of the new request,

Acceptance cost = (3) = $AC_i(T)$

$$= d\left[x_i(1+e)^i + \sum_{j=0}^{S} n_{vij}\left\{\sum_{k=0}^{S} p_{jk}(O_{jk} - c_{jk}) - p_{jA}c_{jA}\right\}\right]\frac{X + x_i}{x_i + \overline{O}_i}$$
$$+ \sum_{j=0}^{S} n_{vij}F_j \tag{5}$$

* B. Lost-sales Cost

Lost-sales cost is measured by contribution made on collection amount, adjusted for incremental cost on credit losses. $LS_i(T)$, lost-sales cost for an i-period-old account, will be

$$LS_i(T) = (1-d)p_{iA}x_i - dp_{iB}x_i + \sum_{j=0}^{S} q_{ij}[(1-d)c_{ij} + VLS_j(T-1)]$$
$$= (1-d)p_{iA}c_{iA} + (1-d)p_{iB}c_{iB} + (1-d)\sum_{j=0}^{S} q_{ij}c_{ij} - (1-2d)p_{iB}c_{iB}$$
$$+ V\sum_{j=0}^{S} q_{ij}LS_j(T-1)$$

$$= (1 - d)EV_i - (1 - 2d)\bar{c}_{iB} + V \sum_{j=0}^{S} q_{ij} LS_j(T - 1), \text{ or}$$

$$LS(T) = (1 - d)EV - (1 - 2d)\bar{c}_B + V.Q.LS(T - 1)$$
$$= (1 - VQ)^{-1}[(1 - d)EV - (1 - 2d)\bar{c}_B]$$
$$= N_v[(1 - d)EV - (1 - 2d)\bar{c}_B]$$

$$LS_i(T) = \sum_{j=0}^{S} n_{vij}[(1 - d)p_{jA}c_{jA} - dp_{jB}c_{jB} + (1 - d) \sum_{k=0}^{S} q_{jk}c_{jk}]$$

However, the expression above includes lost-sales cost on amounts already granted and outstanding, $LS_i'(T)$. Because it is a sunk cost, it should be subtracted from $LS_i(T)$.

$$LS_i'(T) = (1 - d)p_{iA}x_i - dp_{iB}x_i + \sum_{j=0}^{S} q_{ij} \left[(1 - d)c_{ij} + V \left\{ \frac{x_i - c_{ij}}{x_j} \right\} LS_j'(T - 1) \right]$$

Inspection of $LS_i(T)$ and $LS_i'(T)$ reveals that the latter has a coefficient of $\left\{ \frac{x_i - c_{ij}}{x_j} \right\}$ for the recurrence term instead of 1. This is because the current amount outstanding, x_i, will be reduced by c_{ij} instead of being x_j, when it reaches the jth state. If we define

$$c_{ij}' = \frac{x_i - c_{ij}}{x_j}$$

then

$$LS_i'(T) = (1 - d)p_{iA}x_i - dp_{iB}x_i + \sum_{j=0}^{S} q_{ij}(1 - d)c_{ij} + V \sum_{j=0}^{S} q_{ij}' LS_j'(T - 1),$$

where $q_{ij}' = q_{ij}c_{ij}'$ for $i, j = 0, 1, \ldots, S$

In matrix notation,

$$LS'(T) = (1 - d)EV - (1 - 2d)\bar{c}_B + V \cdot Q' LS'(T - 1)$$
$$= (I - V \cdot Q')^{-1}[(1 - d)EV - (1 - 2d)\bar{c}_B]$$
$$= N_{vij}'[(1 - d)EV - (1 - 2d)\bar{c}_B]$$

$$LS_i'(T) = \sum_{j=0}^{S} n_{vij}'[(1 - d)p_{jA}c_{jA} - dp_{jB}c_{jB} + (1 - d) \sum_{k=0}^{S} q_{jk}c_{jk}]$$

Hence, net lost-sales cost, when adjusted for the actual amount of request X,

$$= [LS_i(T) - LS'_i(T)]\frac{X}{\overline{O}_i}$$

$$= \left[\sum_{j=0}^{S} (n_{vij} - n'_{vij})\left\{(1-d)p_{jA}c_{jA} - dp_{jB}c_{jB} + (1-d)\sum_{k=0}^{S} q_{jk}c_{jk}\right\}\right]\frac{X}{\overline{O}_i} \tag{6}$$

III. The Set of Decision-rules

The procedure of formulating the set of decision rules can now be described:

1. Determine policy alternatives (y) other than those concerning extension of credit (acceptance and rejection)—tightening collection efforts, extending the credit period, etc. Determine the number of requests (z) deemed suitable as a sample for an alternative.
2. Grant credit to the total number of requests (yz) determined in (1) and selected at random during a period. Divide the requests, for instance, sequentially into a number of subgroups equal to the number of alternatives (y). Apply each set of policy decisions to one of the subgroups.
3. Determine how you would have classified these requests into predetermined *categories*[3] at each level of investigation. For instance, the information on past experience may be divided into the categories "good," "fair," "poor," and "none."
4. For each policy alternative, construct the following:
   The transition matrix, $[P]$
   The collection-amount matrix, $[C]$
   The collection-cost vector, $\{F\}$
   The current number of accounts in each age category $\{Y\}$
   The current aging of accounts, $\{X\}$[4]
5. Find the acceptance cost and the rejection cost for each time period at the current level of investigation for an alternative. Divide the requests that constituted the basis of (4) into suitable categories according to (3). Weigh the acceptance cost and the rejection cost in proportion to the aging in each category. Determine the set of decision rules at this level of investigation.
6. Apply this set to the requests in the sample. The first time there will be only rejection, if any, but subsequently there may be acceptance or rejection of requests. If there is no change in the composition of acceptance or rejection regions, go to the next step. Otherwise go back to step (4), after modifying the inputs there.
7. When we complete one *level* of investigation, we go to the next level, and go back to step (4). If the original matrices in (4) are modified be-

[3] See Chapter 1.

[4] We may have the new order matrix, O, in place of x, since

$$x_i - c_{ij} + 0_{ij} = x_j, \text{ and } c_{iA} = x_i, \text{ or } x_0 = 0_{00}.$$

cause of the modified sample (owing to requests rejected) the modified versions should now be utilized.

8. If we have completed all levels of investigation, we should find the "further investigation cost" by the iterative process described earlier. On the basis of that, a complete set of decision rules should now be available.
9. When we apply this set to the original sample, it may lead to revision in the original transition matrix and associated values mentioned in (4). Find the value $\sum_{i=0}^{S} y_i DL_i(T)$ from equation (2).
10. When the above process has been carried out for all alternatives, select the alternative that has the maximum $\sum_{i=0}^{S} y_i DL_i(T)$.

Illustration

A hypothetical problem is solved here to illustrate the procedure outlined above.

We assume a two-stage investigation process: (1) the request is automatically granted; and (2) past experience is investigated so as to determine whether a request belongs in the category "good," "fair," "poor," or "new (no experience)" according to guidelines predetermined by management.

During a particular month, we selected a sample of 105 requests, all of which were granted. The table below was prepared by applying to this sample the procedure for classifying past experience.

TABLE 3–1

Frequency Distribution/Past Experience	F_{00}	F_{01}	F_{0A}	F_{10}	F_{11}	F_{12}	F_{1A}	F_{20}	F_{21}	F_{22}	F_{2A}	F_{2B}	Row Total
Good	7	4	7	3	3	0	6	0	0	0	0	0	30
Fair	2	4	3	8	6	16	4	0	2	2	5	0	52
Poor	0	1	0	0	1	2	0	1	3	2	0	1	11
New	1	1	0	0	1	4	1	1	1	1	0	1	12
Column Total	10	10	10	11	11	22	11	2	6	5	5	2	105

$$[P] = \begin{matrix} 1 & 0 & 0 & 0 & 0 \\ 0 & 1 & 0 & 0 & 0 \\ \frac{1}{3} & 0 & \frac{1}{3} & \frac{1}{3} & 0 \\ \frac{1}{5} & 0 & \frac{1}{5} & \frac{1}{5} & \frac{2}{5} \\ \frac{1}{4} & \frac{1}{10} & \frac{1}{10} & \frac{3}{10} & \frac{1}{4} \end{matrix} \qquad [C] = \begin{matrix} 0 & 0 & 0 & 0 & 0 \\ 0 & 0 & 0 & 0 & 0 \\ 143 & (143) & 143 & 55 & 0 \\ 231 & (231) & 231 & 100 & 60 \\ 275 & (275) & 275 & 110 & 132 \end{matrix}$$

$$(Y) = \begin{matrix} 100 \\ 100 \\ 100 \end{matrix} \qquad (F) = \begin{matrix} \$\ 5 \\ 10 \\ 30 \end{matrix}$$

$$d = 2/3$$

$$p_{ij} = \text{payment probability}$$
$$c_{ij} = \text{collection amount}$$
$$y_i = \text{current number of accounts}$$
$$f_i = \text{collection expense}$$

Let $e = .02$ per period

$$V = \frac{1}{1 + e} = \frac{50}{51}$$

$$V \cdot Q = \begin{matrix} 0.32 & 0.32 & 0.00 \\ 0.20 & 0.20 & 0.33 \\ 0.10 & 0.23 & 0.25 \end{matrix}$$

$$[N_v] = (I - VQ)^{-1} = \begin{matrix} 1.81 & 0.90 & 0.47 \\ 0.63 & 1.88 & 0.97 \\ 0.50 & 0.85 & 1.76 \end{matrix}$$

From these input data, the following results are derived through equation (2):

Cash Flows

$$DL_0(T) = 93.49$$
$$DL_1(T) = 94.76$$
$$DL_2(T) = 56.85$$

$$\sum_{i=0}^{2} y_i DL_i(T) = \$(9349 + 9476 + 5685) = \$24{,}510$$

Acceptance and Rejection Costs

If X is the amount of new request, the following costs are derived by using equations (5) and (6):

TABLE 3–2

	Acceptance Cost	Rejection Cost
1. No investigation	$0.10(X + 214^*) + 29.40$	$0.88X$
2. Current	$0.07(X + 143) + 13.98$	$0.84X$
1 month old	$0.09(X + 231) + 29.24$	$0.88X$
2 months old	$0.14(X + 275) + 52.95$	$0.95X$

* Average outstanding balance = .29(143) + .52(231) + .19(275) = 214; note that x_i in equation (5) is equal to c_{iA}.

From this information, we can construct the following table:

TABLE 3–3

			Breakeven Value	
	Acceptance Cost	Rejection Cost	of X	$X + x_i$
1. No investigation	$0.10X + 50.80$	$0.88X$	$65	$279*
2. Past experience				
Good	$0.08X + 29.40$**	$0.85X$	$37	$215
Fair	$0.09X + 52.65$	$0.88X$	$67	$291
Poor	$0.12X + 74.20$	$0.93X$	$92	$343
New	$0.11X + 59.28$	$0.89X$	$76	$307

* X + Average outstanding balance = 65 + 214 = 279.
** $.6(.07X + 23.99) + .4(.09X + 50.03) = .08X + 29.40$.

It seems implausible to infer, for example, that a "poor" account should be extended credit if the outstanding balance *plus* the new request *exceeds* $342, but we should note that the contribution margin is $(1 - d = 1/3)$ and the collection expenditure is a fixed (and significant) amount irrespective of the size of collectable amount. It is, moreover, likely that delinquency of payment is associated with insignificant, small outstanding balances.

The breakeven analysis, when applied to our sample, leads to the following revision of Table 3–1 and associated values of $[P]$ and $[C]$.

TABLE 3–4

Frequency Distribution/Past Experience	F_{00}	F_{01}	F_{0A}	F_{10}	F_{11}	F_{12}	F_{1A}	F_{20}	F_{21}	F_{22}	F_{2A}	F_{2B}	Row Total
Good	7	4	7	3	3	0	6	0	0	0	0	0	30
Fair	2	3*	3	8	6	16	4	0	2	2	5	0	51
Poor	0	1	0	0	1	2	0	1	2*	1*	0	0*	8
New	1	1	0	0	1	3*	1	1	1	1	0	1	11
Column Total	10	9	10	11	11	21	11	2	5	4	5	1	100

* Decrease in the number of accounts because the breakeven criterion is not net.

$$[C] = \begin{matrix} 0 & 0 & 0 & 0 & 0 \\ 0 & 0 & 0 & 0 & 0 \\ 147 & (147) & 147 & 60 & 0 \\ 235 & (235) & 235 & 100 & 62 \\ 318 & (318) & 318 & 120 & 160 \end{matrix} \qquad (F) = \begin{matrix} \$\ 5 \\ 10 \\ 30 \end{matrix}$$

$$[P] = \begin{matrix} 1 & 0 & 0 & 0 & 0 \\ 0 & 1 & 0 & 0 & 0 \\ \frac{10}{29} & 0 & \frac{10}{29} & \frac{9}{29} & 0 \\ \frac{11}{54} & 0 & \frac{11}{54} & \frac{11}{54} & \frac{21}{54} \\ \frac{5}{17} & \frac{1}{17} & \frac{2}{17} & \frac{5}{17} & \frac{4}{17} \end{matrix} \qquad VQ = \begin{matrix} 0.33 & 0.31 & 0.0 \\ 0.20 & 0.20 & 0.39 \\ 0.12 & 0.38 & 0.24 \end{matrix}$$

$$[N_v] = (1 - VQ)^{-1} = \begin{matrix} 1.84 & 0.88 & 0.45 \\ 0.72 & 1.86 & 0.95 \\ 0.55 & 0.83 & 1.73 \end{matrix}$$

Cash Flows

$$DL_0(T) = \$107.11$$
$$DL_1(T) = \$116.68$$
$$DL_2(T) = \$\ 92.93$$
$$\sum_{i=0}^{2} y_i DL_i(T) = \$31{,}672.$$

TABLE 3–5

	Acceptance Cost	Rejection Cost
Current	$0.05X + 20.82$	$0.93X$
1 month old	$0.07X + 45.07$	$0.89X$
2 months old	$0.10X + 83.75$	$1.10X$

Comparison of Tables 3–3 and 3–6 indicates that the breakeven point in terms of the size of the request is lowered for all categories. If we assume that all requests that were rejected after the first run still remain rejected, the system achieves stability.

The next step is to find the "cost of further investigation," assuming

TABLE 3–6

	Acceptance Cost	Rejection Cost	Breakeven Amount	
			X	$X + x_i$
Good	$0.06X + 30.52$	$.92X$	\$35	\$218
Fair	$0.08X + 47.77$	$.94X$	56	291
Poor	$0.09X + 61.27$	$1.00X$	67	332
New	$0.08X + 54.63$	$.98X$	61	310

perfect knowledge. The administrative cost of evaluating the past experience is assumed to be \$1.00. If the request plus the outstanding balance is not greater than \$218, a request will be rejected upon investigation, no matter what category it belongs to. Hence, the cost under consideration will be

$$.30\,(\text{Good} - \text{reject}) + .51\,(\text{Fair} - \text{reject}) + .08\,(\text{Poor} - \text{reject}) + .11\,(\text{New} - \text{reject}) + \text{administrative cost}$$

$$= .30(0.92X) + .51(0.94X) + .08(1.00X) + .11(.98X) + 1.00, \text{ for } X \leq 35$$

$$= .95X + 1.00, \text{ for } X \leq 35$$

Similar computations for other values of X and other relevant information are represented schematically in Figure 3–1.

If our criterion is selection of the lowest-cost alternative, we find

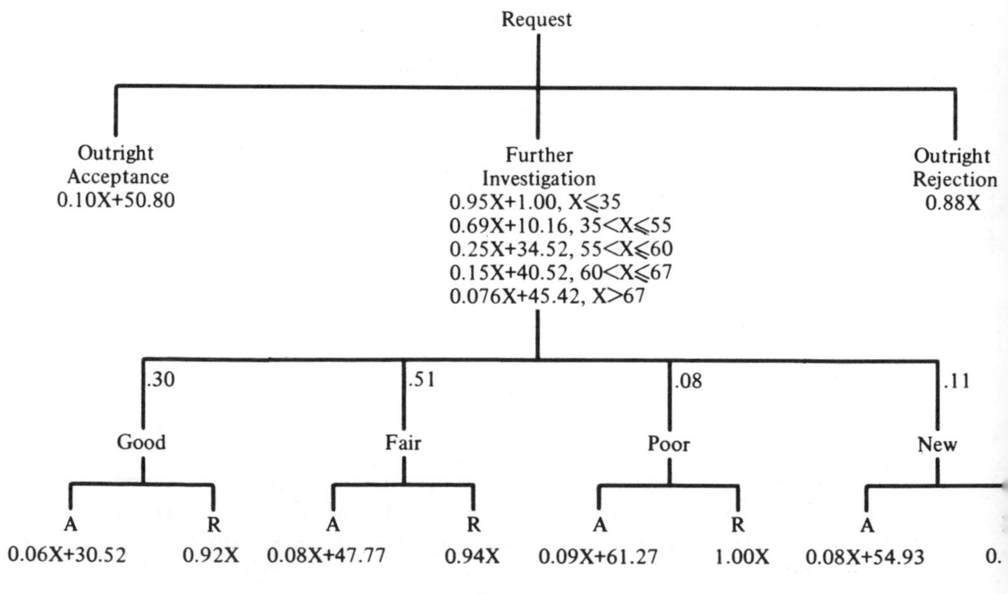

Figure 3–1

that for $0 < X \leq 53$, outright rejection, and $X > 53$, further investigation, alternatives should be selected. Thus, the set of decision rules will be as follows:

1. If a request is not greater than $53.00, reject it outright. A request greater than $332 should be accepted outright.
2. If the request is greater than $53.00, investigate outright the past experience.
   a. If the amount of outstanding balance *plus* the request is less than $218, reject it.
   b. If the amount of outstanding balance *plus* the request is greater than $332, accept the request.
   c. If the request belongs to the category "good," "fair," "poor," or "new," accept it only if the outstanding balance upon the latest credit extension exceeds $218, $291, $332, and $310 respectively.

Even though the rules above can be stated in terms of either the amount of the request alone *or* the amount of outstanding balance *plus* the request (which is conceptually more acceptable), it is felt that the method adopted here is more useful. For instance, if we want to know the oustanding balance of a request at the "no investigation" stage, we may as well know our past experience. All subsequent states (here, for instance, the "past experience" categories) need to take into account both the outstanding amount and the current request. In this connection a paradox should be noted: outright acceptance of a request greater than $65 is suggested in Table 3–3. Similarly, Table 3–6 indicates that a request larger than $67 should be accepted, no matter what category of past experience it belongs to. Why should we undertake further investigation for a request larger than $67? This is because the profitability of credit extension is calculated on the basis of both the current request and the outstanding amount. Thus a request can be larger than $67, and still the outstanding amount upon the request approval may be less than $217.

Another incongruity between the decision tree and the set should be noted. Outright acceptance is always ruled out by the cost figures; however, the set of decision rules suggests outright acceptance of a request greater than $332. First, given our figures, this large a request seems highly unlikely. Second, and more significantly, further investigation has (during the second run of our example) filtered out requests that would otherwise have been accepted: thus, it has raised the rejection cost for the screened sample and lowered its acceptance cost.

IV. Control Indices

Management is interested in two aspects of evaluation:

1. Is lower management carrying out the policy as given by the set of decision rules?
2. Are the results of the policy according to anticipation?

We shall ignore here the behavioral aspects of conscious violation of rules by lower management and assume that decision rules are carried out at lower levels without exceptions.

In order to evaluate the results of a policy, we need indices that will be signals for attention by management in unanticipated situations. These indices are:

1. Bad-debt experience and collections
2. Lost-sales cost
3. Collection expenditure
4. Receivables investment

* A. Bad-debt Experience and Collections

If an account is i-period old now, the probability of its eventually becoming a credit loss will be $BD_i(T)$, where

$$BD_i(T) = p_{iB} + \sum_{j=0}^{S} q_{ij} BD_j(T-1)$$

Or, in matrix notation,

$$\begin{aligned} BD(T) &= p_B + QBD(T-1) \\ &= p_B + Q[p_B + QBD(T-2)] \\ &= p_B + Qp_B + Q^2BD(T-2) \\ &= (I-Q)^{-1}p_B \\ &= Np_B \\ BD_i(T) &= \sum_{j=0}^{S} n_{ij} p_{jB} \end{aligned} \tag{7}$$

The interpretation of equation (7) is straightforward. (n_{ij}) represents the number of times an i-period-old account will be j-period old before it is eventually absorbed either by being fully paid or by becoming a credit loss. The probability of being a credit loss in the jth state is (p_{jB}). Hence the product $(n_{ij}p_{jB})$ summed for all possible value of j will give us the long-run probability of bad debt.

Similarly, if $EP_i(T)$ represents the eventual probability of payment, then

$$EP_i(T) = \sum_{j=0}^{S} n_{ij} p_{jA} \tag{8}$$

If the current aging of accounts is represented by the vector X^p,[5] the bad-debt experience and the average collections will be given, respectively, by

$$\sum_{i=0}^{S} X_i^p \left[\sum_{j=0}^{S} n_{ij} p_{jB} \right] \tag{9}$$

and

$$\sum_{i=0}^{S} X_i^p \left[\sum_{j=0}^{S} n_{ij} p_{jA} \right] \tag{10}$$

B. Lost-sales Cost

Our sample, associated with the efficient alternative, gives us the proportion of the number (and the amount) of incoming requests refused when the corresponding set of decision rules has been applied. The number (and the amount) of requests refused will be given simply by extrapolating the number and the amount of sample requests on a company-wide basis. Both or either of these statistics may be used by management as a surrogate for lost-sales cost.

C. Collection Expenditures

Collection expenditure will depend upon the number of accounts in each aging category. If we have w "new"[6] accounts, the number of times they will be j-period old is n_{0j}. Or wn_{0j} will be the number of j-period-old accounts in the long run. Hence, collection costs per period will be given by

$$\sum_{j=0}^{S} wn_{0j}F_j \tag{11}$$

D. Receivables Investment

If we have H_i, the average size of an i-period-old account (the sample estimates may be adequate), the overall aging of accounts will be directly given by

$$wn_{0j}H_j \quad \text{for } j = 0, 1, \ldots, S \tag{12}$$

It should be noted that *a priori* no one index is superior to other indices for control purposes. A lower level of collection expendi-

---

[5] The superscript p is added here to distinguish the company-wide aging from the sample one defined earlier by x.

[6] An account that has been fully paid and has remained inactive for at least one period—as well as an account that is granted the credit request for the first time—is defined here as a "new" account.

tures, or a smaller number of credit requests refused, or both, would tend to lower the size of collections, lengthen the credit period, increase the bad-debt level, or all three. A smaller number of credit requests refused will tend to raise the collection efforts when an attempt is made to maintain the collections, bad-debt experience, and the receivables investment near the estimated levels. When all policy measures have been followed, only a change in circumstances or underlying assumptions will lead to unanticipated estimates. If changes in circumstances, such as sales, have been responsible, a revision in the estimates leading to changes in the decision rules[7] may be necessary.

Illustration

Assume that, when we have applied the decision rules given in the previous illustration, Table 3–4 still remains valid. Then, control indices will be based upon input data of the second run.

$$(I - Q)^{-1} = N = \begin{matrix} 1.89 & 0.93 & 0.49 \\ 0.77 & 1.92 & 1.01 \\ 0.59 & 0.88 & 1.78 \end{matrix}$$

Bad-debt experience, from equation (7), is given by

$$\begin{aligned} BD_0 &= (1.89)(0) + (0.93)(0) + (0.49)(0.06) \\ &= 0.029 \\ BD_1 &= 0.061 \\ BD_2 &= 0.107 \end{aligned}$$

Payment probabilities, from equation (8), are given by

$$\begin{aligned} EP_0 &= 0.971 \\ EP_1 &= 0.939 \\ EP_2 &= 0.107 \end{aligned}$$

Collection expenditure, from equation (11), is given by

$$w[(1.89)(5) + (0.93)(10) + (0.49)(30)]$$

$= 33.45w$, where w = the number of "new" accounts (see footnote 6).

[7] Control limits wherein fluctuations of indices are permissible can be computed through sensitivity analysis described in Chapter 1.

Aging, from equation (12), will be

Current	$w(1.89)(147)$	$= 277.83w$
One-month	$w(0.93)(235)$	$= 218.55w$
Two-month	$w(0.49)(318)$	$= 155.82w$

V. Conclusion

Credit extension and collections are two major aspects of credit management. In this chapter, we have interrelated the decision-tree approach to appraising individual credit requests and the Markov process for selecting collection policy by means of an iterative procedure. This effort not only enables us to devise decision-making rules accounting for dynamic relationships among factors influencing and influenced by credit management but also provides us with control indices for evaluating implemented policy alternatives.

Part Two

INVENTORY MANAGEMENT

Just as decisions on credit granting and collections affect the level of investment in accounts receivable, decisions with regard to the acquisition (or production) of goods affect the inventory investment. However, the financial manager is generally not in charge of production or purchasing in a large organization. As a result, he is not directly connected with inventory management. Nevertheless, since inventory investment requires allocation of financial resources, *overall* inventory levels are of direct concern to the financial manager.

A desirable inventory level can be easily achieved either through an excessively large number of purchasing orders (or very small production runs of individual products) or by keeping customers' demand unfulfilled for abnormally long periods of time. Such practices adversely affect funds generated by operations. Consequently, the financial manager is concerned with (1) overall inventory levels, in conjunction with (2) the number and size of orders (or ordering cost), and (3) the number and size of unfulfilled orders (or lost-sales cost).

Chapter 4 deals with inventory management under certainty. Chapter 5 removes the assumption of certainty and focuses attention on single-item and multiple-item inventories. Decision rules are formulated under (1) a fixed-order system requiring perpetual inventory accounting and (2) a fixed-period system dealing with periodic inventory accounting. Subsequently, these decision rules are linked with evaluation indices related to inventory levels, orders, and lost sales (or back orders).

Inventory Management under Certainty

I. Introduction

ACQUISITION or production of goods precisely when demand for them materializes is economically unwise, if not physically impossible. Backlogging orders and filling them as goods become available is also a questionable practice in a competitive economy. A normal practice is to make acquisitions in anticipation of demand and thereby create inventories, because inventories obviate the need for a precise synchronization of acquisition and demand.

There are two basic questions concerning inventories:

1. When should we place an order for acquisition?
2. What should be the size of the order?

For a known level of demand (or its distribution), solution of one question also resolves the other. For instance, a large frequency of orders (or a short period of time between two consecutive orders) implies a small order size each time. This relationship has led to two basic types of inventory systems: the fixed-order system and the fixed-period system. Under a fixed-order system, the size of the order remains the same but the timing of orders may vary. In a fixed-period system, on the other hand, orders of varying sizes are placed at regular intervals of time. In this chapter, we shall study the inventory systems under the assumption of a known *level* of demand. In Chapter 5, we shall assume a known probability *distribution* of demand, i.e., demand under conditions of "risk."

It should be noted at the outset that there is extensive literature on inventory management, covering a wide variety of situations.[1] However, this literature is not directly relevant to the financial manager. Inventory levels are affected by sales and acquisitions. Sales are externally determined in inventory models. As a result, acquisitions are the sole *decision* variables in this literature. Because the financial manager in a large organization is not in direct charge of production or purchasing, his viewpoint differs from that of the existing models. Furthermore, in order to give insight into a variety of demand situations or acquisition patterns, these models typically focus upon inventory management of a single item. But the financial manager is concerned with *aggregate* inventory investment and its effect on fund flows generated by the firm. Therefore the manager requires the devising of aggregate evaluation indices pertaining to a *multi-item* inventory system.

Because aggregate evaluation indices should be logically linked with operating decisions, we cannot construct these indices without devising optimal decision rules for the items held in inventory. This necessitates a discussion of some selected conventional models that construct decision rules incorporating the production (or purchasing) manager's viewpoint. In order to facilitate exposition, we will first describe the relevant costs related to inventory decisions. Second, we will deal with single-item inventory situations. Third, we will discuss the distinctive characteristics of a multi-item inventory system; and, finally, we will analyze the issue of devising the aggregate indices.

II. Relevant Costs

There are three types of cost[2] to be considered:

1. The *setup* cost
2. The *investment* (or carrying) cost
3. The *shortage* cost

The *setup cost* (also known as the "procurement cost") includes costs associated with such things as preparing the order and making changes in machine setups for production runs. An important characteristic of the setup cost is that its magnitude is not affected by the size of the

---

[1] As a matter of fact, there exist books exclusively devoted to inventory management; e.g., Starr and Miller [1962], Hadley and Whitin [1963], and Naddor [1966].

[2] We are excluding here costs associated with devising and implementing the inventory *system*.

order.[3] Hence, the per-unit setup cost decreases as the size of the order increases.

The *investment cost* includes the cost of capital or return on the foregone opportunity; storage cost; obsolescence, deterioration, and pilferage charges; and insurance charges. The investment cost is incurred as soon as an item is put into inventory, and its size is determined by the duration for which the item remains in inventory. Often this cost is not strictly dependent upon the size of inventories per unit of time. For instance, heating and lighting costs for a warehouse of a given size may not fluctuate with changes in the size of inventories. Nevertheless, for convenience, they may be treated as a continuous function of size.

The *shortage cost* is associated with the situation where demand cannot be fulfilled in a normal fashion because of insufficient inventories. If the demand is fulfilled by measures such as special production runs or procurement orders, the costs of such expediting measures are included in the shortage cost. Frequently, unfilled demands are backlogged and no attempt is made to satisfy them by any special action. In this case, the customer may decide to take his business elsewhere either temporarily or permanently. Costs associated with such actions are also known as "lost-sales" costs or "lost goodwill" costs.

Needless to say, costs are defined here in terms of avoidable opportunity cost; thus, only controllable costs are relevant for our purposes.

III. Basic Single-Item Models

A. The EOQ Model

The fixed order size or EOQ (economic-order-quantity) model for inventory management is perhaps the most frequently encountered model in the literature and in practice. Basically, this model operates under the following assumptions:

1. Constant demand rate, per unit of time
2. Deterministic (known with certainty) environments with respect to demand and cost
3. Insignificant or nonexistent lead time between placing an order and receiving the goods ordered
4. Unlimited cash available for inventory investment

Let us suppose that

D = Demand, in physical units, for the period under consideration

[3] Costs that are dependent upon the size of the order are conventionally lumped together with the unit cost. Transportation cost or inspection cost, associated with the size of the order, is thus prorated and included in the cost per unit.

s = Setup cost per order

i = Investment cost per dollar for the period under consideration

Q = Quantity for each order, in physical units

p = Unit cost

Tc = Total cost for the inventory system

In this case, the number of orders for the entire period [4] will be given by $\frac{D}{Q}$ (note that Q is still unknown). Then the total setup cost will be

$$\$\left(s \cdot \frac{D}{Q}\right)$$

Because the lead time between ordering and receiving goods is insignificant and demand is known with certainty, shortages cannot occur. We therefore would have no reason to maintain a safety stock.

Each time we order Q units, consequently, given the constant demand rate, the inventory of Q units would deplete at a constant rate.

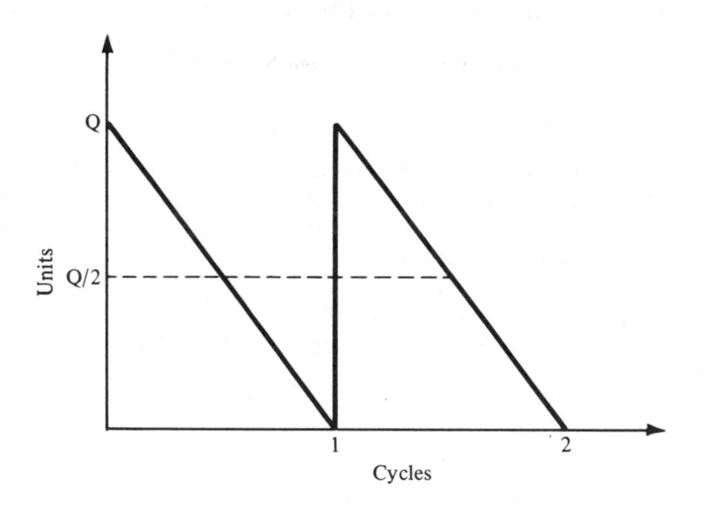

Figure 4–1. Behavior of Inventories over Time

Then, the *average* inventories would be $\left(\frac{Q}{2}\right)$ units for the interval between two consecutive orders, as is shown in Figure 4–1. Or, equiva-

[4] This period is typically a year; however, other appropriate time lengths may be used.

lently, the average inventories for the entire period will be $\left(\frac{Q}{2}\right)$ units. Hence, the investment cost will be \$ $\left(i \cdot \frac{pQ}{2}\right)$, where \$$(pQ)$ is the value of the order.[5]

The total cost (Tc) is simply the sum of the ordering cost and investment costs, and will be given by

$$Tc = \left(s \cdot \frac{D}{Q}\right) + \frac{ipQ}{2} \tag{1}$$

Our interest is in minimizing this total cost, and the unknown variable is Q. Then, differentiating (1) with respect to Q, and equating the resultant expression with zero, we get

$$-\frac{sD}{Q^2} + \frac{ip}{2} = 0$$

or

$$Q^* = \left[\frac{(2sD)}{ip}\right]^{1/2} \tag{2}$$

where Q^* = the optimal quantity per order.

It should be noted that i and D are stated for the same length of time. For instance, if demand is related to a six-month period, i should be the investment cost per dollar for the six-month period. Also, both D (demand) and Q (the order quantity) are stated in terms of physical units.

The following aspects of the *EOQ* model are noteworthy.

1. INVENTORY-SALES RELATIONSHIPS

Economic-order-quantity provided by equation (2) may be restated as

$$Q^* = \left(\frac{2s}{ip}\right)^{1/2} \cdot (D)^{1/2} \tag{2'}$$

Because s, i, and p are known constants, we naturally find that the optimal value of Q depends upon sales. What is surprising, however, is that Q (and, consequently, the average inventory size) is not a linear function of sales but a square-root function of sales. Thus, if demand were to quadruple, average inventories would only double in size. This result is a serious warning against the indiscriminate use of ratio analysis.

---

[5] The unit cost, p, will naturally be the appropriate incremental cost here.

One may question the validity of the argument against ratio analysis on the grounds that the optimality condition in equation (2) is based upon simplified but unrealistic assumptions. However, for the most part, as we shall see later, changes in these assumptions do not change the basic relationship between average inventories and sales.

2. SENSITIVITY ANALYSIS

Often, the strength of a model is determined by the stability of the optimal solution in terms of errors in parameter estimates. Our parameters are the demand level for the period and the cost estimates for the investment setup. Suppose that one of these values is incorrectly measured. To what extent would this error change the optimal quantity Q^* in equation (2)? We need not undertake an elaborate analysis[6] because the impact of a parameter is clear. *Overestimating* the demand or setup cost would *increase* the average inventory level by the square root of the magnitude of the error. *Underestimating* the investment cost would lead to a similar *increase* in the average inventory level. From these observations, it follows that if both the setup cost (or demand) and the investment cost are overestimated by the same magnitude, the two overestimations will cancel each other out, and the optimal solution will not be affected.

There is one interesting although obvious implication of the sensitivity analysis for the financial manager. When he suspects that demand is overestimated, he can prevent overinvestment in inventories by providing a higher estimate of the investment cost or a lower estimate of the setup cost.

3. ORDERING TIME

Let us consider now the problem of placing the optimal number of orders. In this case, we want to determine the optimal timing between two consecutive orders.

Let N be the unknown number of orders within a given time period. Let all previous assumptions with respect to demand and cost characteristics, as well as lead time, still hold. In that case, the total cost will have only two components:

1. Investment-storage cost
2. Order cost

The order size would be $\left(\frac{D}{N}\right)$ units, and the average inventory would be $\left(\frac{D}{2N}\right)$ units. The value of average inventories would be $\$\left(\frac{D}{2N} \cdot p\right)$.

---

[6] For a rigorous analysis, see Starr and Miller [1962, pp. 176–181].

Thus, the investment cost will be

$$\$\left(\frac{D}{2N}\cdot p\right)i \tag{3}$$

Similarly, the order cost will be

$$\$(N)(s) \tag{4}$$

Hence, the total cost will be given by

$$\text{Total cost} = \text{order cost} + \text{investment cost}$$

$$Tc = Ns + \frac{iDp}{2N} \tag{5}$$

Differentiating equation (5) with respect to N, and setting the resultant expression equal to zero to get the minimum cost, we obtain

$$s - \frac{iDp}{2N^2} = 0$$

or

$$N^* = \left(\frac{iDp}{2s}\right)^{1/2}$$

If we divide D by N^*, provided by the equation above, we get

$$\frac{D}{N^*} = Q^* = \left(\frac{2sD}{ip}\right)^{1/2}$$

This is precisely the value provided by equation (2). Because determining the economic order-size quantity also determines the number of orders, we shall concentrate only on problems of economic order size in this chapter.

B. Relaxation of the Assumptions of the EOQ Model

As we have seen above, the *EOQ* model is based upon the following assumptions:

1. The lead time is negligible, and orders are filled at once.
2. The demand is constant and known.
3. Unit cost, p, is constant—i.e., no quantity discounts.
4. Unlimited funds are available for investment in inventories.

We shall relax the first three assumptions in this section. The impact of relaxing the last assumption will be taken up during our discussion of multi-item inventories (see "Investment Constraint," beginning on page 93).

1. LEAD TIME

Lead time is given by the interval between placing an order and receiving the goods ordered. An inventory cycle is defined by the interval between receipts of two consecutive orders. Given these definitions, we find that there are two different situations:

1. Lead time is smaller than the cycle.
2. Lead time is larger than (or equal to) the cycle.

When the lead time is significant but smaller than the cycle, we can no longer order the economic quantity precisely at the point when our inventories are depleted. If the lead time is constant and known, our task is considerably simplified. Suppose the lead time is L units of time. In that case, the demand during the lead time would be

$$\left(D \cdot \frac{L}{T}\right) \text{ units}$$

where D is the demand for T, the period under consideration. We should, then, place our order when the size of the inventories is $\left(\frac{D \cdot L}{T}\right)$ units. The optimal order size will still be the same as that given by equation (2).

It should be noted that L and T have the same dimension: for instance, if the lead time is expressed in months, T should also be stated in terms of months (rather than weeks or years).

When the lead time is larger than the cycle, we find that the economic order quantity will still be the same. The only difference from the previous situation is that there would be at least one order outstanding all the time; in the previous situation, an order would be outstanding only during the lead time. This has some significance, as we shall see later, for indices constructed for management control. For systems evaluation, we will be interested not only in inventories on hand but also in the quantity on order that has not been delivered.

Up to this point, relaxing the assumption with respect to lead time by itself has not affected the size of the economic order quantity. However, when the assumption of certainty is also relaxed, we find that lead time has a significant impact on the order quantity (this situation will be examined in Chapter 5).

Often orders are not filled at once; instead, they are filled at a constant rate over a period of time. Let this rate be q per unit of time. Now, our lead time is L. Then, if Q is the quantity to be ordered for a cycle, $(q \cdot L)$ is equal to Q.

Since we have so far assumed demand to be constant throughout the cycle, we will deplete the inventories during the lead time at a constant rate. Let us define this rate as d per unit of time. Then $\frac{Q}{d}$ would give us the length of the inventory cycle.

Because goods are flowing into inventories at the rate q, and out of inventories at the rate d, the *net* rate of inflow is $(q - d)$ during the lead time L. Thus, by the end of the lead time, we will accumulate inventories given by the quantity

$$(q - d)L$$

Note that $q > d$; if this were not so, we would not have any inventory. These inventories would deplete at a constant rate throughout the cycle. This situation is presented in Figure 4–2, which enables us to calculate

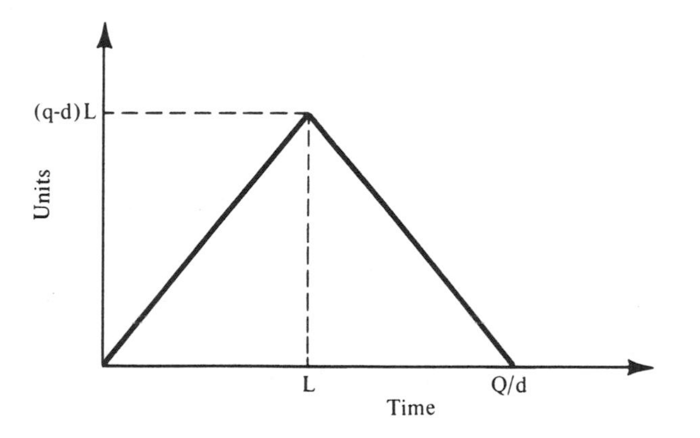

Figure 4–2. Inventory Cycle for Noninstantaneous Order Fulfillment

the *average* inventories during the inventory cycle. This value is given by the area of the triangle represented by the heavy lines, divided by the length of the cycle. The area of the triangle is given by

$$\frac{1}{2} \cdot \frac{Q}{d} (q - d)L$$

The length of the cycle is given by

$$\frac{Q}{d}$$

Thus, the average inventories will be

$$\frac{1}{2}(q - d)L$$

Because $(q \cdot L) = Q$, we may express average inventories by the expression

$$\frac{1}{2}Q\left(1 - \frac{d}{q}\right)$$

Then, the investment cost will be

$$\$\left[\frac{1}{2}ipQ\left(1 - \frac{d}{q}\right)\right]$$

and the order cost will be

$$\$\left(s \cdot \frac{D}{Q}\right)$$

as before. Thus, the total cost, Tc, will be given by

$$\text{Total cost} = \text{order cost} + \text{investment cost}$$

$$Tc = s \cdot \frac{D}{Q} + \frac{ip}{2}Q\left(1 - \frac{d}{q}\right) \tag{6}$$

Differentiating Tc with respect to Q and setting the resultant expression equal to zero to obtain the optimal value of Q, we get

$$Q^* = \left[\frac{2Ds}{ip(1 - d/q)}\right]^{1/2} \tag{7}$$

A comparison between this expression and equation (2) indicates that the denominator of the basic equation is adjusted by the factor of $\left(1 - \frac{d}{q}\right)^{1/2}$. The optimal order quantity would be larger in the current case because $\left(1 - \frac{d}{q}\right)$ is positive and less than 1.

Notice that, for practical purposes, unless deliveries are stretched out over a long period of time, the approximation of the optimal order quantity provided by equation (2) would be reasonably accurate. The order size and, as a result, inventories, would be smaller by a factor of $1 \Big/ \left(1 - \frac{d}{q}\right)^{1/2}$ in that case.

2. DEMAND RATE

So far we have assumed that the demand rate is constant throughout the planning period. Often, however, the demand rate is not constant over time. To what extent does such a behavior affect inventory management? We shall examine this question for two cases. The first case assumes an increase in the demand at a constant rate; in this case, we shall look at the economic-order-quantity model. The second case deals with fluctuating demand; to deal with this situation, dynamic programming will be utilized.

* *a. Increasing demand.*[7] Let r_t be the demand rate at instant t. If demand increases linearly over time, we may express

$$r_t = at \qquad a > 0;\ 0 \leq t \leq T \tag{8}$$

As before, let

D = demand for the entire planning period

N = the number of inventory cycles in the planning period

Q = the economic order size

i = investment cost per unit

p = unit cost

s = setup cost

Tc = total cost

Naturally,

$$\begin{aligned} Tc &= \text{ordering cost} + \text{investment cost} \\ &= Ns + ip\ (\text{average inventory}) \end{aligned}$$

Our problem, then, is to determine average inventory over time.

Consider the planning period to be T time units long. Since demand during the entire period is D,

$$\begin{aligned} D &= \int_0^T r_t\,dt \\ &= \int_0^T at\,dt, \text{ from (8)} \end{aligned}$$

[7] This section draws heavily on the power pattern for demand and its implication for inventories in Naddor [1966], pp. 111–114.

$$= \left[\frac{at^2}{2}\right]_0^T$$

$$= \frac{aT^2}{2}$$

or,

$$a = 2D/T^2$$

and

$$r_t = 2Dt/T^2 \qquad (8')$$

As is shown in Figure 4–3, if we are to acquire D units at the begin-

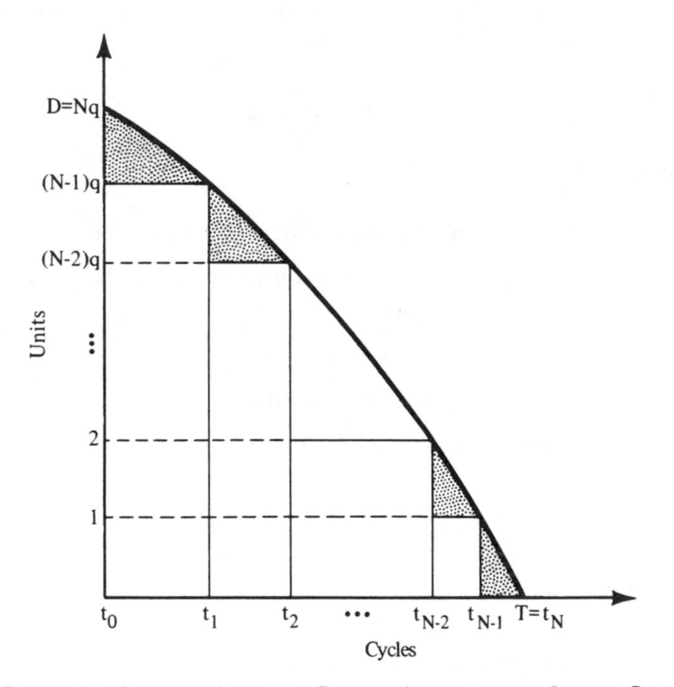

Figure 4–3. Inventory Levels for Demand Increasing at a Constant Rate

ning of the planning period, the inventory level is given by the parabola. Because this area represents one-half of a regular parabola, the area representing inventory under the present condition will be

$$\frac{1}{2}\left(\frac{4}{3}DT\right) = \frac{2}{3}DT$$

We do not, however, order the entire demand of D units initially. Instead, we order it in N installments of Q units. This being the case, the entire inventory can be represented by the shaded area in Figure 4–3. Thus, during the first cycle, the total inventories would be given by

[the segment of the parabola between 0 and t_1 abscissa]
– [the rectangle with the same base & height of $(N - 1)q$]

The quantity in the first bracket is given by

$$\frac{2}{3} DT - \frac{2}{3} (N - 1)q \ (T - t_1)$$

The quantity in the second bracket is

$$(N - 1)q \cdot (t_1 - t_0)$$

Hence, the total inventories during the *first* cycle will be

$$\frac{2}{3} DT - \frac{2}{3} (N - 1)q(T - t_1) - (N - 1)q(t_1 - t_0).$$

Similarly, for the *second* cycle, the total inventories will be

$$\frac{2}{3} (N - 1)q(T - t_1) - \frac{2}{3} (N - 2)q(T - t_2) - (N - 2)q(t_2 - t_1)$$

and so on.

Then the total inventories during N cycles will be

$$\frac{2}{3} DT - \sum_{i=1}^{N-1} (t_i - t_{i-1})(N - i)Q \tag{9}$$

We know that $Q = \frac{D}{N}$. Thus our task is to simplify further the second term on the right side of equation (9).

Since we do not permit any back orders or lost sales,

$$\begin{aligned} Q_i = Q &= \int_{t_{i-1}}^{t_i} r_t \, dt \\ &= \int_{t_{i-1}}^{t_i} \frac{2Dt}{T^2} \, dt, \text{ from equation (8')} \\ &= \frac{D}{T^2} (t_i^2 - t_{i-1}^2) \end{aligned}$$

i.e.,

$$Q = \frac{D}{N} = \frac{D}{T^2} (t_i^2 - t_{i-1}^2)$$

Or:

$$\frac{T^2}{N} = (t_i^2 - t_{i-1}^2)$$

Because $t_0 = 0,$

$$t_1^2 = T^2/N$$

$$t_2^2 = T^2/N + t_1^2$$

$$= 2T^2/N$$

and $t_3^2 = T^2/N + t_2^2$

$$= 3T^2/N$$

Or, in general

$$t_i^2 = iT^2/N \qquad \text{for } i = 1, 2, \ldots, N$$

i.e., $t_i = T(i/N)^{1/2}$

Plugging this value of t_i and t_{i-1} into equation (9), we get

$$\text{Total inventories} = \frac{2}{3}DT - D\sum_{i=1}^{N-1}(1 - i/N)T[\sqrt{i/N} - \sqrt{(i-1)/N}]$$

Dividing this expression by the length of the period, and rearranging, we get the *average* inventories, I. Thus

$$I = D\left\{\frac{2}{3} - \frac{1}{\sqrt{N}}\sum_{i=1}^{N-1}(1 - i/N)[\sqrt{i} - \sqrt{(i-1)}]\right\}$$

$$= D\left\{\frac{2}{3} - \sqrt{\frac{(N-1)}{N}} + \frac{1}{N\sqrt{N}}\sum_{i=1}^{N-1}[i\sqrt{i} - i\sqrt{(i-1)}]\right\}$$

$$= D\left\{\frac{2}{3} - \frac{1}{\sqrt{N}}[N\sqrt{(N-1)} - (N-1)\sqrt{(N-1)} + \sqrt{(N-2)} + \cdots + \sqrt{2} + \sqrt{1}]\right\}$$

$$= D\left\{\frac{2}{3} - \frac{1}{\sqrt{N}}[\sqrt{(N-1)} + \sqrt{(N-2)} + \cdots + \sqrt{2} + \sqrt{1}]\right\}$$

$$= Df(N), \text{ where}$$

$$f(N) = \frac{2}{3} - \frac{1}{\sqrt{N}}[\sqrt{1} + \sqrt{2} + \cdots + \sqrt{(N-1)}] \tag{10}$$

Our total cost will be given as

$$\text{Total cost} = \text{order cost} + \text{investment cost}$$

$$Tc_N = sN + ipDf(N)$$

The optimal value of N given by N^* would be such that

$$Tc_{N^*} \leq Tc_{N^*+1}$$

and

$$Tc_{N^*} \leq Tc_{N^*-1}$$

Thus,

$$ipDf(N^*) + sN^* \leq ipDf(N^* + 1) + s(N^* + 1)$$

i.e.,

$$ipD[f(N^*) - f(N^* + 1)] \leq s$$

i.e.,

$$\frac{ipD}{s} \leq \frac{1}{f(N^*) - f(N^* + 1)} \tag{11}$$

Similarly,

$$ipDf(N^*) + sN^* \leq ipDf(N^* - 1) + s(N^* - 1)$$

leads to

$$\frac{ipD}{s} \geq \frac{1}{f(N^* - 1) - F(N^*)} \tag{12}$$

From (11) and (12), we get

$$\frac{1}{f(N^* - 1) - f(N^*)} \leq \frac{ipD}{s} \leq \frac{1}{f(N^*) - f(N^* + 1)} \tag{13}$$

where $f(N^*)$ is defined by equation (10).

For computation purposes, i, p, D, and s, are parameters whose values are provided. Once we compute the value (ipD/s), we will select the N^* that satisfies the inequality given by equation (13). This value of N^* will be optimal, and the corresponding value of Q^* will be given by (D/N^*).

Here is an example:

Let

$$D = 1{,}200 \text{ units}$$

$$s = \$20$$

$$p = \$10$$

$$i = .10$$

$$T = 1 \text{ year}$$

Then,

$$\frac{ipD}{s} = 60$$

$$\frac{1}{f(N-1) - f(N)} \leq 60 \leq \frac{1}{f(N) - f(N+1)}$$

where $$f(N) = \frac{2}{3} - \left(\frac{\sqrt{1} + \sqrt{2} + \cdots + \sqrt{N-1}}{\sqrt{N}}\right)$$

for $N = 6$, $f(N-1) = .117$, $f(N) = .0963$, and $f(N+1) = .0819$

Then,

$$\frac{1}{f(N-1) - f(N)} = \frac{1}{.0207} \doteq 48$$

$$\frac{1}{f(N) - f(N+1)} = \frac{1}{.0144} \doteq 69$$

Thus

$$N = 6, \quad \text{and} \quad Q = \frac{1200}{6} = 200 \text{ units.}$$

If we had used the basic *EOQ* model,

$$Q = \left(\frac{2sD}{ip}\right)^{1/2} = (2 \times 20 \times 1200)^{1/2} \doteq 219 \text{ units}$$

Or, the order size would have been 10 percent larger than the optimal order size.

b. Uneven demand and dynamic programming. Linearly increasing demand is not the situation most commonly encountered in practice. However, its handling does suggest a way of attacking problems where demand exhibits a "regular" pattern. Often, we do encounter cases where demand is known but remains uneven over time. Commonly observed rules of thumb, such as 30-day orders, are not necessarily optimal; nor is the basic *EOQ* model applicable without putting the demand pattern into a straitjacket. A *computational* technique called "dynamic programming" is extremely useful in such situations.

Suppose we are told that demand for a product during the last four months of the year is as follows:

September	40 units
October	75 "
November	30 "
December	50 "

Assume that

1. Orders are placed on the first day of each month and are instantaneously filled.
2. Demand occurs on the first day of the month, and delays are not permitted.
3. There are no initial inventories.
4. There should not be any ending inventories.

The first two assumptions enable us to avoid computing the average inventories during a month. The last two assumptions are made here only for convenience.

Let $i = .01$ per month

$$p = \$100$$

$$s = \$100$$

A basic tenet of dynamic programming is that optimal decisions in later periods dictate decisions to be made in earlier periods, so that these may be consistent with the consequences of the earlier decisions and the overall policy is optimal. Even though this sounds intuitively appealing, the task of computing can become formidable in light of the exponential number of possible combinations. What dynamic programming offers is, as we shall see below, a computational convenience rooted in rationality. For this purpose, let us turn now to our example. Consider, initially, the month of September. Since we do not have any initial inventory, we have no choice but to order the desired quantity for September. For an order of 40 units the total cost for September would be \$100 because there would not be any inventory investment cost.

Now, for the month of October, we have two decision alternatives:

1. Order in September a sufficiently large quantity to cover the demand for October. In this case, we will incur an inventory cost in September of (\$1 × 75), plus the order cost of \$100.
2. Order in October as if the optimal September decision had been carried out. In this case, we have the ordering cost of \$100 for October, and the optimal (only) decision in September costs us \$100.

Thus, we find that the first alternative, defined as (9–10), would cost us \$175, and the second alternative, defined as (9;10), would cost us \$200. Hence, considering two months together, we find (9–10) optimal.

Similarly, for November, we have three alternatives:

1. (9–11): Order in September to cover the demand through November. In this case, the ordering cost will be only \$100. However, we will carry inventories of the demand for October in the month of September, and of

the demand for November in both September and October. Thus our inventory investment cost would be

$$\$1[1 \times 75 + 2 \times 30] = \$135$$

giving a total cost of $235.

2. (10–11;9): Order for October and November together, and follow the optimal policy for September. The optimal policy for September costs us $100. The October–November policy would cost us $100 (the order cost) *plus* $30 (inventory investment cost during October); hence the total cost would be $130 for October-November. And the total cost for (10–11; 9) will be

$$\$130 + \$100 = \$230$$

3. (11;10): Order in November as if the optimal decision for the period up to (and including) October had been made. The latter period would cost us $175, as we have seen above. The November order costs us $100. Hence, the total cost of (11;10) would be $275.

On the basis of these considerations, we find that the alternative represented by (10–11;9) is optimal; that is, the least expensive alternative will be ordering in September for September alone, and ordering in October for October–November.

A similar line of reasoning for December would require us to consider four alternatives:

1. (9–12): Order in September to cover demand for the entire four-month period.
2. (10–12;9): Order in October for the remaining three months, and follow the optimal policy for September.
3. (11–12;10): Order in November for November–December, and follow the optimal policy for the period up to October.
4. (12;11): Order in December for December alone, and follow the optimal policy for the preceding period.

Table 4–1 gives us the costs associated with different lengths of time.

TABLE 4–1 Policies

September(9)	October(10)	November(11)	December(12)
$100	(9–10)*$175 (9;10)$200	(9–11)$235 (10–11,9)*$230 (11;10)$275	(9–12)$385 (10–12;9)$330 (11–12;10)*$325 (12;11)$330

It follows from these cost estimates that when we consider the four-month period as a whole, we should order in November for the November–December period and follow the optimal policy for the period preceding November. In other words, order in September and November to cover the demand for a two-month period.

Certain characteristics of this numerical procedure should be noted. First, it forces our attention to the fact that what is an optimal policy for a planning period of a given length may not be optimal for a different planning period. If, for instance, we considered demand for only the September–November period, we would have placed orders in September and October. But in the four-month period, we will not consider ordering anything during October. An important corollary of this observation is that we must exercise great care in selecting a planning period of a proper length. This task, however, is not so formidable as it sounds because cyclical *demand* patterns, typically encountered, suggest the use of a complete demand cycle as an appropriate planning period. Even when such cyclical patterns are not easily discernible, we do not have to consider more than eighteen periods for practical purposes.[8]

Second, a question arises with respect to the computational procedure: Must we consider all the alternatives available for each state period? Fortunately, the answer is no. The cost characteristics often enable us to eliminate otherwise acceptable alternatives from further consideration. For instance, we could have ignored the first alternative under the heading "December" in Table 4–1, because saving the ordering cost of $100 is far outweighed by the 50 units in inventory carried for the December demand: the resultant investment cost is $50 per month for September, October, and November. We would, then, have to compute the costs of only three alternatives.

Finally, the efficiency of the computational procedure becomes clearer as we move toward the planning horizon. For instance, there are a number of strategies associated with different combinations. Again, going back to Table 4–1, we find that under the alternative of ordering in December and following the optimal policy for September–October–November, there is no need to repeat the calculations for September–October–November. Thus, we did not again consider the question of whether to order in September and November or September and October. Instead, the systematic procedure allowed us to select the optimal solution for the period preceding December.

3. QUANTITY DISCOUNTS

Many times, the supplier offers a discount in the purchase price per unit for quantity buying. When the optimal quantity determined by the basic *EOQ* model is *larger* than the minimum quantity qualifying for a lower unit price, we are simply reaping an additional benefit, and in this case we need not review our purchasing policy. A policy review is necessary when the optimal purchase order is *smaller* than the minimum quantity necessary for the lower unit price. In this event, purchasing this minimum quantity has costs and benefits. Benefits are

[8] cf., Boot [1967], p. 123.

provided by the discount itself and by the lowered order cost for the period under consideration because the number of orders would be smaller. On the other hand, the average inventories and the associated investment cost would increase. We consider buying the minimum quantity for discount only when benefits outweigh the cost.

Consider the following example:

$$D = 80{,}000 \text{ units}$$
$$i = .10$$
$$p = \$10$$
$$s = \$100$$

If our order is for at least 5,000 units, we are given a 10 percent discount; i.e., $p_d = \$9$ for an order of 5,000 units or more.

At the regular price

$$Q^* = \left(\frac{2sD}{ip}\right)^{1/2} = 4{,}000 \text{ units}$$

$$\text{Total cost} = \text{order cost} + \text{investment cost}$$

$$\text{Total cost} = \$100 \times \frac{80{,}000}{4{,}000} + \frac{4{,}000}{2}(.10)(\$10)$$
$$= \$4{,}000.$$

If we are to use $p = \$9$,

$$Q_d^* = \left(\frac{2 \times 80{,}000 \times 100}{.1 \times 9}\right)^{1/2} = 4{,}216 \text{ units}$$

If the revised quantity Q_d^* was 5,000 or more units, the answer would have been to take advantage of the discount policy. In our case, we need to calculate further the total cost to determine whether the firm should take advantage of the discount. If we are to buy the minimum quantity of 5,000 units, we will place 16 orders per planning period, and the average inventories will be 2,500 units for this period. Thus,

$$\text{Total cost} = \$100 \times 16 + 2{,}500(.10)(\$9)$$
$$= \$3{,}850.$$

Hence, we should take advantage of the discount policy by ordering the minimum quantity each time.

In summary, as long as we retain the basic premise of certainty, the basic single-item inventory models contain assumptions with respect to behavior of demand and cost that can be relaxed without any great difficulty.

IV. Multi-item Considerations

Our discussion so far has been confined to inventory management problems for a single item. Most organizations, however, deal with more than one item. Are there any unique problems in handling inventories of more than one item?

Prima facie, it appears that whatever has been said so far should be valid for each and every item. Hence, a multi-item inventory can be handled by applying the basic model to each item, and the overall policy will consequently be a sum of policies for individual items.

Even though that argument is reasonable, we find many important instances where individual policies are not necessarily consistent with the overall optimality. Often, new problems crop up that are either nonexistent or insignificant for a single-item inventory. For instance, gathering cost information pertaining to different items may take a long time; or there may be restrictions on the overall level of investment in inventories; or we may procure more than one item from a single supplier. In these instances, we find that our analysis must be modified to a certain extent.

We shall investigate these modifications for the following situations:

1. When information on ordering cost and investment cost is not available and gathering it would take considerable time or effort.
2. When there is an aggregate investment constraint on inventories.
3. When a group of items are supplied by one vendor.

A. The Multi-item Inventory and Lack of Information on Costs

When we do not have any knowledge of the magnitude of the investment cost or setup cost, the model under consideration provides us with useful information to improve the inventory situation.

Consider, again, equation (2):

$$Q = \left(\frac{2sD}{ip}\right)^{1/2}$$

It can be restated as

$$Q = \left(\frac{2s}{i}\right)^{1/2} \left(\frac{D}{p}\right)^{1/2}$$

$$= k \left(\frac{D}{p}\right)^{1/2} \quad \text{where} \quad k = \left(\frac{2s}{i}\right)^{1/2} \tag{2'}$$

Now, the number of orders, N, during the period under consideration, is given by

$$N = \frac{D}{Q}$$

Substituting the value of Q from equation (2′), we get

$$N = \frac{D}{k}\left(\frac{p}{D}\right)^{1/2}$$

$$= \left(\frac{Dp}{k^2}\right)^{1/2} \tag{14}$$

If we have m items in our inventories, the total number of orders will be given by

$$\sum_{j}^{m} N_j = \sum_{j}^{m} \frac{1}{k_j} (D_j p_j)^{1/2}$$

It is reasonable to assume that these costs do not differ for different products because we have no knowledge of investment or setup cost. For instance, it may be likely that a group of items requires a higher insurance rate, owing to a greater fire hazard; but if we lack such knowledge, it is fair to assume that k_j remains constant for all items.

Then
$$\sum^{m} N_j = \frac{1}{k} \sum^{m} (D_j p_j)^{1/2}$$

or,
$$k = \frac{\sum^{m} (D_j p_j)^{1/2}}{\sum^{m} N_j} \tag{15}$$

Once we determine the value of k in this fashion, we may employ equation (2′) to find the optimal order size, and thereby the average inventory level. The following example illustrates this procedure.

We have the following data for four products:

Item	Units Sold = D	Unit Cost = p	# of Orders Currently = N
A	1,000	$ 5	10
B	500	20	10
C	400	10	8
D	200	8	4

From this information, we find that

Item	\$ Demand = Dp	$(Dp)^{1/2}$	Order Size = Qp	Average Inventory = $\frac{Qp}{2}$
A	5,000	\$ 70.70	\$ 500	\$250
B	10,000	100.00	1,000	500
C	4,000	63.25	500	250
D	1,600	40.00	400	200

$$\text{Total inventory investment} = \$1{,}200$$

$$\sum N_j = 32$$

$$\sum (D_j p_j)^{1/2} = \$273.95$$

Then, from equation (15),

$$k = \frac{273.95}{32} = 8.56$$

Utilizing equation (2′), we get a revised order quantity, Q', for each item as well as associated average inventories and the number of orders as shown below:

Item	$(D/p)^{1/2}\, k = Q'$	$Q'p$	Average Inventory = $\frac{Q'p}{2}$	N'
A	(14.14)(8.56) = 121	\$605	\$303	8
B	(5.00)(8.56) = 43	860	430	11
C	(6.32)(8.56) = 54	540	270	8
D	(5.00)(8.56) = 43	344	172	5

$$\text{Total inventory investment} = \$1{,}175$$

$$\sum N_j' = 32$$

Thus we reduce inventories by \$25 with the same number of orders.

B. Investment Constraint

Consider now inventory management of m items subject to an investment ceiling of \$$K$ on average inventories. Since the average inventory of an item is represented by

$$\frac{Q}{2}$$

this restriction suggests that

$$K \geq \sum_{j=1}^{m} \frac{Q_j p_j}{2} \tag{16}$$

where p_j = the unit cost for the jth item.

If we apply our basic model and find that the average aggregated inventories are less than \$$K$, we can conclude that the policy restriction is not critical, and it is not binding. In other words, if the restriction imposed by expression (16) were binding, the restriction would be reduced to an equality, i.e.:

$$K = \sum_{j=1}^{m} \frac{Q_j p_j}{2} \tag{17}$$

This equation can also be written as

$$K - \sum_{j=1}^{m} \frac{(Q_j p_j)}{2} = 0 \tag{18}$$

Now, our objective function in the form of the total cost is given by

$$\text{Total cost} = \text{order cost} + \text{investment cost}$$

$$Tc = \sum_{j=1}^{m} \frac{s_j D_j}{Q_j} + \frac{1}{2} \sum_{j=1}^{m} i p_j Q_j$$

If we multiply the left side of equation (18) by an unknown quantity z and add the resultant expression to the total cost function, Tc will not change because (18) is equal to zero. Thus,

$$Tc = \sum_{j=1}^{m} \left[\frac{s_j D_j}{Q_j} + \frac{i p_j Q_j}{2} \right] + z \left[K - \sum_{j=1}^{m} \left(\frac{Q_j p_j}{2} \right) \right]$$

In order to minimize the total-cost function, we differentiate the above function with respect to Q_j and z and set the derivatives equal to zero. These simultaneous equations give us:

$$Q_j = \left[\frac{2 s_j D_j}{p_j (i - z)} \right]^{1/2} \quad \text{for } j = 1, 2, \ldots, m \tag{19}$$

Substituting this value into equation (18) provides us with

$$z = i - \frac{\sum_j (s_j p_j D_j / 2)^{1/2}}{K} \tag{20}$$

Now, z would be a negative quantity and is known as a "Lagrangian multiplier," or, in economic terms, a "shadow price" for the capital constraint. Its interpretation is simple: If we are to alleviate our capital constraint by \$1, the incremental returns will be worth $\$(-z)$. On the other hand, if our constraints were $\$(K - 1)$, the total cost associated with inventories would increase by $\$z$.

This interpretation of z has one major implication for management. When we are dealing with various forms of assets, economic theory suggests that we should invest in each form to the extent that the shadow prices for capital invested in different assets are the same for all forms of assets. Thus the investment to be allocated among, say, inventories and accounts receivable should be such that $z_{\text{inventories}}$ is equal to $z_{\text{receivables}}$. In this fashion, then, we avoid arbitrary upper limits for investment in different forms of assets.

There are, however, some conceptual and practical problems to be resolved. First, i is the investment cost; to the extent that z is not zero, the implication is that i is inaccurately estimated. Or, to put it differently, if i is correctly measured, the allocation of resources would be such that providing an artificial, arbitrary constraint would be unnecessary; the value of z will be zero. This reasoning is correct; and to the extent that we superimpose an arbitrary constraint on inventories *alone,* a misallocation may result. Notice, however, that equation (19) has in the denominator $p_j(i - z)$. Management, then, can either superimpose the capital constraint or increase the required rate of return, i, by the amount $(-z)$. In practice the former method is often preferred, because its rationalization is easier. Moreover, i incorporates, among other things, the cost of capital. This cost is measured for a longer period of time than the typical life of an item in inventory. For instance, i may be measured in terms of expected returns for the duration of the firm, and as we have noted earlier, inventories typically have life spans of less than a year. Periodic or seasonal cycles that can vitally affect inventory management may have little or insignificant impact on the capital cost. In this sense, the capital constraint would more appropriately reflect the swings or cycles and would obviate the need for continual periodic revision of the capital-cost estimate.

A practical problem should not be overlooked. Our analysis for handling capital restriction requires a continuous cost function that is differentiable. Often, cost functions are discontinuous. For instance, raising \$10 million in debt capital may cost us a 10 percent interest rate; however, \$15 million in debt capital can be raised only at a stiff rate of 30 percent in terms of effective cost. Fortunately, however, we are not likely to run into such a problem as regards inventory management.

Finally, it should be noted that our method of handling the capital restriction can be easily adapted to handling other restrictions. For instance, we may have limited machine capacity for production,[9] or we

[9] See Buchan & Koenigsberg [1963, pp. 319–323].

may want to restrict the number of orders.[10] In such cases, the Lagrangian-multiplier method facilitates the solution procedure.

C. Various Items from One Supplier

Many times a supplier provides a number of items. Intuitively, it is obvious that if we are to process all these items in one order, the ordering cost would be defrayed over a large number of items, and may even outweigh any increased inventory cost.

Consider that m items are purchased from a supplier.

Let
$$\sum_{j=1}^{m} p_j D_j = \$K$$

Now, if these items were individually purchased, the optimal order would be

$$Q_j^* = \left(\frac{2sD_j}{ip_j}\right)^{1/2} \quad \text{for } j = 1, 2, \ldots, m$$

The total cost would be:

$$\text{Total cost } (j^{\text{th}} \text{ product}) = \text{order cost } (j^{\text{th}} \text{ product}) + \text{investment cost } (j^{\text{th}} \text{ product})$$

$$Tc_j = \frac{sD_j}{Q_j} + \frac{ip_jQ_j}{2}$$
$$= sD_j\left(\frac{ip_j}{2sD_j}\right)^{1/2} + \frac{ip_j}{2}\left(\frac{2sD_j}{ip_j}\right)^{1/2}$$
$$= (2siD_jp_j)^{1/2}$$

Thus, for all m items, the total cost would be:

$$\sum_j Tc_j = (2si)^{1/2} \sum_j (p_jD_j)^{1/2} \tag{21}$$

If we were to treat all these m items together, for

Q_p = the *value* of an order, we would have:

$$Tc = s\left(\sum_j D_jp_j/Q_p\right) + \frac{i}{2}Q_p$$

---

[10] See Starr & Miller [1962, pp. 97–98].

Or: $$Tc = \frac{sK}{Q_p} + \frac{iQ_p}{2}, \qquad \text{where } K = \sum D_j p_j$$

Then, $$Q_p^* = \left(\frac{2sK}{i}\right)^{1/2}$$

Substituting this value of Q_p in the total cost relationship, we get

$$\begin{aligned} Tc &= \frac{sK(i)^{1/2}}{(2sK)^{1/2}} + \frac{i}{2}\left(\frac{2sK}{i}\right)^{1/2} \\ &= (2siK)^{1/2} \\ &= (2si)^{1/2}\left(\sum_j D_j p_j\right)^{1/2} \end{aligned} \tag{22}$$

Comparison of equations (21) and (22) indicates that

$$\sum_j Tc_j > Tc$$

if $$(2si)^{1/2} \sum_j (p_j D_j)^{1/2} > (2si)^{1/2}\left(\sum_j p_j D_j\right)^{1/2}$$

i.e., $$\sum_j (p_j D_j)^{1/2} > \left(\sum_j p_j D_j\right)^{1/2} \tag{23}$$

Let $m = 2$, $p_1 D_1 = a^2$, and $p_2 D_2 = b^2$. Then the left side of the inequality (23) will be $(a^2)^{\frac{1}{2}} + (b^2)^{\frac{1}{2}} = (a + b)$ and the right side of the inequality will be $(a^2 + b^2)^{\frac{1}{2}}$.

Now, $(a + b) > (a^2 + b^2)^{\frac{1}{2}}$ because

$$(a + b)^2 > (a^2 + b^2) \quad \text{for } a > 0, \quad b > 0.$$

(a and b represent our demand for items 1 and 2 in dollar terms; hence, they cannot be negative.) A similar line of reasoning can show us that the inequality holds for $m > 2$.

Thus we find that when we are ordering more than one item from a supplier, it pays to consider these items together in terms of their usage. Note that this usage is expressed in dollars so as to represent a homogeneous dimension for adding purposes. Moreover, whether the *physical* usage of an item is low or high will not be significant for our purposes.[11]

So far we have discussed the impact of a multi-item inventory system

[11] This statement needs a qualification. When ordering an item requires a review that costs money (say, a physical check), the ordering cost does not remain constant for the case where we deal with aggregated dollar usage. See Starr and Miller [1962, pp. 106–108]. Note, however, that under our present assumption of deterministic, uniform demand, the review cost need not be significant.

on optimal decision rules for ordering. When there are many items in the inventory, management also wants to evaluate the overall inventory situation. We now turn to this issue.

V. Evaluation of the Inventory System

When we have only one item in inventory, inventory control is not an important issue. This would not be the case for a multi-item inventory. The manager cannot review the implementation of inventory policy, when, say, hundreds of items are involved. Moreover, the position of the financial manager is peculiar with respect to inventory management: even though he is not directly in charge of inventories in a typically large organization, his raising of funds often impinges upon the state of inventories, and thereby he is held responsible for inventory management. A natural question for him is how to make sure that inventory investments are appropriate.

Suppose that the demand for a firm's m products is fairly certain and remains constant throughout the year. If the inventory policy is based on the EOQ model, the financial manager will have orders of the size

$$Q_j^* = \left(\frac{2sD_j}{ip_j}\right)^{1/2} \quad \text{for } j = 1, 2, \ldots, m.$$

The average inventories will be $Q_j^*/2$, and the inventory turnover ratio in terms of annual usage will be

$$D_j/(Q_j^*/2) \quad \text{for } j = 1, 2, \ldots, m$$

That is:

$$\frac{2D_j}{Q_j^*} = \left[\frac{(2ip_jD_j)}{s}\right]^{1/2}$$

$$= \left(\frac{2i}{s}\right)^{1/2} (p_jD_j)^{1/2}$$

$$\text{Then, } \log \text{ (inventory turnover)} = \frac{1}{2}\log\left(\frac{2i}{s}\right) + \frac{1}{2}\log\,(p_jD_j).$$

Here $\frac{1}{2}\log\left(\frac{2i}{s}\right)$ represents the intercept and $\frac{1}{2}\log\,(p_jD_j)$ the slope of a line on a log paper describing the relationship between the inventory-turnover ratio and the annual usage. Thus the financial manager can make adequate provision for inventory financing, once he is given the annual usage forecasts for different items. He is also able to detect overinvestment quickly by plotting inventory-turnover ratios and the annual usage on a log paper for each item. If ordering costs and inventory investments cost do not differ from item to item, he can easily check to determine whether the aggregate investment in inventory is appropriate rather than checking individual items.

Even when the financial manager is responsible only for inventory investment, he is well advised to look into the overall cost. It is easily possible to hold down inventories by placing an excessive number of orders. Now, we have seen above that

$$\text{Total } \textit{average} \text{ inventories} = \sum_{j=1}^{m} \frac{Q_j^*}{2} = \left(\frac{s}{2i}\right)^{1/2} \sum_{j=1}^{m} (p_j D_j)^{1/2}$$

Similarly,

$$\begin{aligned} \text{Total number of orders} &= \sum_{j=1}^{m} D_j/Q_j^* \\ &= \sum_{j=1}^{m} \left(\frac{i}{2s}\right)^{1/2} (p_j D_j)^{1/2} \\ &= \left(\frac{i}{2s}\right)^{1/2} \sum_{j=1}^{m} (p_j D_j)^{1/2} \end{aligned}$$

Hence,

$$\text{Total average inventory/total number of orders} = \frac{s}{i}$$

The implication of the equation above is clear: the relationship between the aggregate average inventory and the total number of orders is determined by the ratio of the ordering cost to the inventory investment cost.

In brief, the financial manager can look into two sets of indices. First, he can check the inventory-turnover ratio by examining the chart of individual items on a log paper, where items *below* the straight line represent lower inventory turnover. Second, the total number of orders should not exceed the number provided by

$$\frac{i}{s} \text{ (total average optimal inventory)}$$

In practice, we often run into situations where the number of items is so large that it may not be possible for the financial manager to review all items effectively. In such cases, an "A, B, C" classification system is employed to increase the effectiveness of review.

The "A, B, C" classification system is based on the idea of providing attention where it counts. If, for instance, we are dealing with 500 items, we may find that 50 items account for 70 percent of the total usage; another 50 items account for an additional 15 percent of the total usage; and the remaining 400 items account for only 15 percent of the usage. The first 50 items, in this case, belong to group A, the second 50 to group B, and the remaining to group C.

In such a situation, the financial manager should scrutinize closely the individual items in group A; he may classify items in group B into subgroups and provide some attention to the subgroups; and he may pay only cursory attention to items in group C.[12] This reduces his supervision time considerably, and, at the same time, makes his efforts more effective.

VI. Conclusion

In this chapter, inventory systems under certainty were constructed. For this purpose, attention was focused upon single as well as multiple items in inventory. For the single-item inventory, consideration was given to significant lead time, noninstantaneous replenishment rates, and uneven demand rates. For multiple items, investigation of situations such as absence of cost information and budgetary constraints was undertaken. Finally, considerations for the financial manager regarding control were examined in the context of multiple-item inventory.

[12] For theoretical considerations determining classification of items into various groups and subgroups, see Starr and Miller [1962, pp. 181–190].

Inventory System under Uncertainty

I. Introduction

When we no longer assume a demand level known with certainty, the issue becomes what level of demand should be fulfilled and what the corresponding level of inventories should be. When the order size is larger than the expected demand during the relevant period, the excess is known as "safety stock." Thus, when we know only the probability distribution of demand (rather than the exact demand), our central concern is to determine the optimal level of safety stock.

In this chapter, we will first determine safety stock under the assumption that the order size to fulfill the *expected* demand is already determined. Then we will drop this assumption and analyze the interactions between the order size and the safety-stock level. We will undertake this analysis for the fixed-order system (*FOS*) as well as the fixed-period system (*FPS*), because these two basic systems have different implications for the safety stock. As a matter of fact, we find that the safety-stock level under the fixed-period system turns out to be larger than that under the fixed-order system; but this does not indicate that the fixed-order system is superior because other cost considerations, discussed later, must be accounted for in choosing a system. Then, we will examine the (s, S) system, which represents a combination of the two basic systems, under the assumption of discrete demand distribution;

this assumption facilitates the use of the Markov process described in Chapter 2. Finally, we will discuss the financial manager's responsibilities as regards a multi-item inventory system, especially the evaluation of such a system.

II. Safety Stock and the Fixed-order System

A. Determination of Safety Stock Alone

Under the fixed-order system, we place an order of the optimal size as soon as the inventory level reaches a predetermined level. Under deterministic conditions, we find the optimal size of the order by applying the *EOQ* model described in Chapter 4. Similarly, the minimum inventory level for placing an order is determined by the length of the lead time.

If the lead time is zero, random fluctuations in demand or usage obviously can be absorbed without any difficulty. Suppose the optimal size of the order is 100 units to be utilized over a period of 30 days, and we can procure any number of units without any penalty. In that case, even if a random spurt of demand were to exhaust inventories in twenty-five days, instantaneous procurement of goods would still enable us to fulfill demand for the remaining five days (and later) without any penalty. Thus we find that when the lead time is zero, we do not have to hold any safety stock, and the ordering cost remains constant under the fixed-order system. Moreover, we may safely apply the deterministic models of the previous chapter under these conditions.[1]

If the lead time is significant, however, we find that the safety stock does become important. Suppose that the lead time is smaller than the inventory cycle;[2] then we have to determine (1) the optimal order size and (2) the point in time when we should place the order, or the point in time when the *stock on hand* falls to a given level known as the "reorder point." The stock on hand should not only cover the *expected* demand during the lead time but also should include some additional stock to meet demand larger than the expected level. Consider the case where the demand distribution is *normal.* If we do not carry any additional (safety) stock, we would be able to cover the random demand in only 50 out of every 100 inventory cycles. If, on the other hand, management wants to be out of stock only once in 100 cycles, the firm should carry safety stock sufficiently large to provide against fluctuations in demand 99 out of 100 times. In this case, the safety stock and the reorder point are determined in the following way.

---

[1] The only modification will be to replace the known level of demand with the *expected* demand level.

[2] Throughout this chapter, we shall keep this assumption.

Let the expected demand for the entire planning period of T units be $\bar{D}$ and the corresponding standard deviation σ_D. Then the expected value and the standard deviation *per unit of time* will be

$$\frac{\bar{D}}{T} \quad \text{and} \quad \frac{\sigma_D}{(T)^{1/2}}$$

respectively. Now we can derive the optimal order size as in Chapter 4, replacing D with $\bar{D}$.

Suppose that L is the number of time units for the lead time. Then the expected demand during the lead time will be

$$L \cdot \frac{\bar{D}}{T}$$

and the standard deviation will be

$$\sigma_L = \sigma_D(L/T)^{1/2}$$

Inspection of normal distribution tables shows that if we keep the safety stock level at

$$2.33\sigma_L$$

we will not be out of stock 99 times out of 100 cycles in the long run. Thus the reorder point, R, will be given by the sum of the anticipated demand during the lead time and the safety-stock level, i.e.,

$$R = \frac{L \cdot \bar{D}}{T} + 2.33\sigma_D \left(\frac{L}{T}\right)^{1/2}$$

When we determine the safety stock and the reorder point in this way, we are assuming a lack of knowledge about the shortage cost. When we have that knowledge, prescribing the percentage level of stockout is superfluous: knowledge of one contains information for the other. To understand this, let us assume that the shortage cost is $\$u$ per unit of lost demand and the lead-time cost, C_L, will be

$$C_L = (R + \bar{D}_L - \tilde{D}_L)i + (\tilde{D}_L - R - \bar{D}_L)u$$

where $\tilde{D}_L$ is the random demand. In other words, if there is demand for $\bar{D}_L$ units, we have a storage cost of i per unit for the surplus stock and a shortage cost of u per unit for the insufficient stock. The *storage* cost will be incurred as long as $\tilde{D}_L$ is smaller than (or equal to) $\bar{D}_L + R$ units. The *shortage* cost will be incurred if $\tilde{D}_L$ exceeds this number ($\bar{D}_L + R$). Thus the relevant total cost, Tc, will be

$$Tc = \int_0^{\overline{D}_L+R} i(\overline{D}_L + R - x)f(x)\,dx + \int_{\overline{D}_L+R}^{\infty} u(x - \overline{D}_L - R)f(x)\,dx$$

Note that here x refers to the random demand, and the expression $f(x)$ denotes the probability that the actual demand will be x units.

Since the value of R is unknown, the total-cost expression with respect to R will be minimized by differentiating Tc with respect to R and setting the resultant expression equal to zero. Thus,

$$\frac{\partial Tc}{\partial R} = \int_0^{\overline{D}_L+R} if(x)\,dx + i(\overline{D}_L + R - \overline{D}_L - R)f(\overline{D}_L + R)$$

$$- \int_{D_L+R}^{\infty} uf(x)\,dx + u(\overline{D}_L + R - \overline{D}_L - R)f(\overline{D}_L + R)$$

$$= \int_0^{\overline{D}_L+R} if(x)\,dx - \int_{\overline{D}_L+R}^{\infty} uf(x)\,dx = 0$$

That is:

$$iF(\overline{D}_L + R) - u[1 - F(\overline{D}_L + R)] = 0$$

where $F(\overline{D}_L + R)$ represents the cumulative probability of demand for $(\overline{D}_L + R)$ units, or

$$\int_0^{D_L+R} f(x)\,dx = F(\overline{D}_L + R) = \frac{u}{i + u}$$

In our previous example, we wanted to be out of stock only once in every 100 cycles. Thus $F(\overline{D}_L + R) = .99$. Then

$$.99 = \frac{u}{i + u}$$

or:

$$u = 99i$$

when i is 10 percent

$$u = \$9.9$$

Thus the shortage cost is \$9.90 per unit.

B. Determination of Safety Stock and Lot Size

So far we assumed that determination of the optimal Q^* was made before (and independently of) determination of the optimal safety stock, R^*. This may be a reasonable approximation of reality, and a great computational convenience; however, it is not the optimal solution from a conceptual viewpoint, because Q^* and R^* are interrelated.

The significance of the interrelationship between Q^* and R^* may be appreciated if we take the following line of reasoning. In the preceding section, we saw that determination of R^* requires specification of either the shortage cost or the proportion of stockout cycles, and that if one number has been provided, the other is automatically determined. Now the total shortage cost for a given planning period will depend upon the proportion of stockout cycles and the number of cycles in the planning period. Since the number of cycles is inversely related to the quantity Q^*, the total shortage cost will depend upon Q^*. In turn, the total shortage cost is a component of the total relevant cost, which determines Q^*. Thus Q^* determines and is determined by R^*.

It should be noted here that we will confine ourselves to uncertainty in demand; we will ignore uncertainty related to the lead time. In other words, our assumption throughout this chapter is that the lead time is known with certainty. If in reality the lead time takes a random value, it is not unreasonable to reflect this randomness in the demand distribution. Suppose, for instance, that the lead time may be from five to ten days and that demand per day, during the lead time, takes a value between ten and fifteen units. In this case, the lowest value of demand during the lead time would be $5 \times 10 = 50$ units; the highest value will be 150 units; and for *practical purposes,* we may assume the lead time to be exactly seven days. The only reason for this convenient assumption, it should be pointed out, is to avoid still more complex formulations than those we are about to undertake.

The procedure for deriving the optimal quantities Q^* and R^* involves two steps: first, define the total-cost function; and, second, apply minimization calculus rules to it. The total-cost function will now be composed of three elements:

1. Ordering cost
2. Carrying cost (inventory investment cost)
3. Stockout cost

If we order Q quantity each time, we will have N orders during a given planning period, where

$$N = \frac{\overline{D}}{Q}$$

That being the case, the total ordering cost will be

$$\$s \cdot N \tag{1}$$

Because we are carrying R units of safety stock to meet random fluctuation in the lead-time demand, it is likely that *on the average* we will carry R units in stock. Note that just before the reorder point, our inventories will be

$$\overline{D}_L + R = r$$

units, where $\overline{D}_L$ is the *expected* lead-time demand. Thus, when the ordered quantity Q arrives, sometimes we may have $\overline{D}_L + R$ units in stock (if there is no demand at all), and at other times our stock may have been depleted before the new order arrives. Since on the average the lead-time demand will be for $\overline{D}_L$ units, by definition, in the long run when the ordered quantity arrives we will have $\overline{D}_L + R - \overline{D}_L = R$ units in stock. If, for convenience, we assume that the rate of usage or demand remains constant, our *average* inventories will be

$$\frac{Q}{2} + R$$

units. Or, to state this quantity in terms of N, we will have

$$\frac{\overline{D}}{2N} + R$$

units on average in stock. Since p is the cost in terms of dollars per unit; and i is the inventory investment cost per dollar *per planning period,* the total inventory investment cost will be

$$ip\left[\frac{\overline{D}}{2N} + R\right] \tag{2}$$

or

$$ip\left[\frac{\overline{D}}{2N} + r - \overline{D}_L\right] \tag{3}$$

As in the preceding section, we assume that stockout cost per unit of unfulfilled demand is $\$u$. Suppose that the demand during a particular lead time is x units, for $x \geq r$. Because we will not be able to fulfill demand for $(x - r)$ units, the stockout cost will be

$$\$u(x - r)$$

Now x can take any value above or equal to r. If $f(x)$ describes the probability that the demand will take a particular value x, then the *expected* stockout cost per cycle will be

$$\int_r^\infty u(x - r)f(x)\,dx$$

Since we have N cycles in the planning period, the *total* expected stockout cost will be

$$\$Nu \int_r^\infty (x - r)f(x)\,dx \tag{4}$$

Now the total cost will be given by

Total cost = order cost + investment cost + shortage cost

$$Tc = sN + ip\left[\frac{\overline{D}}{2N} + r - \overline{D}_L\right] + uN\int_r^\infty (x - r)f(x)\,dx \tag{5}$$

Here we have two unknowns to be determined: N and r. (Note that our original unknowns, Q and R, are here transformed in N and r through known parameters only for notational convenience.) Then a partial differentiation of the total-cost function with respect to N and r respectively, and setting the resultant expressions equal to zero, will provide us with two simultaneous equations, with two unknowns, whose solution will be the desired quantities N^* and r^*.

Now

$$\frac{\partial Tc}{\partial N} = s - \frac{ip\overline{D}}{2N^2} + u\int_r^\infty (x - r)f(x)\,dx = 0 \tag{6}$$

$$\frac{\partial Tc}{\partial r}[3] = ip + uN\left[-(r - r)f(r) - \int_r^\infty f(x)\,dx\right]$$

$$= ip - uN\int_r^\infty f(x)\,dx = 0 \tag{7}$$

Now a cumulative probability function $F(x)$ is defined as

$$F(x) = \int_0^x f(y)\,dy$$

Then, we can restate equation (7) as

$$ip - uN[1 - F(r)] = 0$$

or,

$$ip - uN + uNF(r) = 0$$

---

[3] The partial differentiation of an integral is given by the following

If $$g(x) = \int_x^\infty xg(y)\,dy,$$

then $$\frac{\partial g(x)}{\partial x} = \int_x^\infty g(y)\,dy - xg(x)$$

i.e.,
$$-F(r^*) = \frac{ip - uN^*}{uN^*} \tag{8}$$

If we let
$$G(r) = \int_r^\infty (x - r)f(x)\,dx, \tag{9}$$

equation (6) can be written as

$$s - ip\frac{\overline{D}}{2N^2} + uG(r) = 0$$

i.e.,
$$\frac{1}{N^*} = \left[\frac{2s + 2uG(r)}{ip\overline{D}}\right]^{1/2}$$

and
$$Q^* = \frac{\overline{D}}{N^*} = \left\{\frac{2\overline{D}[s + uG(r)]}{ip}\right\}^{1/2} \tag{10}$$

Equations (8), (9), and (10) form the system that provides the optimal solution for Q^* and r^*. Obviously, the value of r^* is not explicitly stated for the following reasons: first, it is the cumulative value of the probability function that is known; second, even this cumulative function depends upon the optimal value N^*, or Q^*, and Q^* cannot be found unless the value of r^* is known because the numerator of Q^* contains a term $G(r^*)$. In other words, the solution procedure will be iterative: a trial-and-errror method will be necessary to derive the optimal values.

Before we demonstrate the trial-and-error method, two matters should be mentioned that facilitate it.

First, we shall assume that the demand has a normal distribution. In particular, let the mean for the lead-time demand be $\overline{D}_L$ and the corresponding standard deviation be σ. Then, as is shown in the Appendix to this chapter,

$$\begin{aligned} G(r) &= \int_r^\infty (x - r)f(x)\,dx \\ &= \sigma\phi\left(\frac{r - \overline{D}_L}{\sigma}\right) + (\overline{D}_L - r)\left[1 - F\left(\frac{r - \overline{D}_L}{\sigma}\right)\right] \end{aligned}$$

where $\phi(x)$ represents the ordinate of the normal density function, and $F(x)$ represents the cumulative normal distribution. Tabulations of these values are found in any standard statistical text. The task of computation, then, is made easier.

Second, from the inspection of equation (10), it is apparent that $Q^* \geq Q$ (basic). When either $u = 0$ or $G(r) = 0$, Q^* is equal to Q (basic). It is easy to show why $Q^* \geq Q$ (basic). The number of back orders is inversely related to r^*: if the safety stock is large enough, there will be no back orders. Similarly, the stockout cost is inversely related to Q^*; a larger Q^* implies a smaller number of cycles, and hence a smaller stockout cost. Then, by increasing the Q (basic), we offset the increased inventory investment cost more than adequately by a decrease in the back-order cost. Computationally, this characteristic is of immense help because the trial-and-error method is set into motion by the approximation of Q^* by Q (basic). This value, in turn, enables us to compute $F(r^*)$, given in equation (8). The value of r^* derived in this fashion will enable us to compute $G(r^*)$ in equation (9), and in turn, equation (10) will now give us the value of Q^*, which will replace the value of Q (basic) in the first step; we will repeat this procedure until the initial Q^* is the same as Q^* derived in the final step. This procedure may sound cumbersome and involved, but it really is not. In fact, two or three provisional values of Q^* soon converge to the optimal Q^*, as is shown in the following example.

Example:

$$
\begin{aligned}
\text{Let } \bar{D} &= 1{,}200 \text{ units} \\
D_L &= 100 \text{ units} \\
i &= 0.10 \\
\sigma &= 20 \\
p &= \$100 \text{ per unit} \\
u &= \$150 \text{ per unit} \\
s &= \$1{,}000 \text{ per order}
\end{aligned}
$$

1.

$$
\begin{aligned}
Q\text{ (basic)} &= \left(\frac{2\bar{D}s}{ip}\right)^{1/2} \\
&= \left[\frac{2 \times 1.200 \times 1.000}{(.10)(100)}\right]^{1/2} \\
&= 490 \text{ units}
\end{aligned}
$$

This is the first provisional value of Q^*.

$$N = \frac{\bar{D}}{Q^*} = \frac{1.200}{490} = 2.45$$

2. From equation (8),

$$F\left(\frac{r^* - 100}{20}\right) = \frac{ip - uN^*}{uN^*}$$

From Normal tables, we find that

$$\frac{r^* - 100}{20} = 1.92$$

or:

$$r^* = 138.4$$

3. $$G(r^*) = 20\phi(1.92) + (100 - 138.4)[1 - F(1.92)]$$
$$= .2183$$

4. $$Q_1^* = \left\{\frac{2 \times 1{,}200[1{,}032.745]}{(.10)(100)}\right\}^{1/2}$$
$$= 498 \text{ units}$$

or

$$N_1^* = 2.41$$

5. Repeating step 2, we get

$$F\left(\frac{r^* - 100}{20}\right) = \frac{iP - uN^*}{uN^*}$$

Whence $$r^* = 138.3$$

6. Then

$$G(r^*) = 20\phi(1.92) + (100 - 138.4)[1 - F(1.92)]$$
$$= .2183$$

and

7. $$Q_2^* = 498 \text{ units}$$

Thus the optimal order size will be 498 units; the optimal safety stock will be 38 units; and an order should be placed as soon as the stock on hand is 138 units.

Note that under the basic system, the optimal order size is 490 units. If we had the policy of a 5 percent stockout level (i.e., to be out of stock once in every 20 cycles) then,

$$r = D_L + 1.96\ (\sigma)$$
$$= 100 + 1.96\ (20)$$
$$= 139 \text{ units.}$$

Thus it can be seen that the approximation provided by the basic formula for the optimal order size and the reorder point is not unreasonable in this case.

III. Safety Stock and the Fixed-period System

A. Determination of Safety Stock Alone

Under the fixed-period system, the inventory situation is reviewed periodically and a decision is made as to whether to order and how much to order. Under the deterministic conditions of Chapter 4, decision rules under the fixed-period system did not differ from those under the fixed-order system. However, this is no longer the case when demand is not known with certainty.

To appreciate the difference between two systems under the assumption of uncertainty, let us first recall some pertinent definitions. First, we defined *inventory cycle* as the time interval between receipt of two consecutive orders. The inventory cycle is also given by the time interval between two consecutive reviews because we assume throughout that the lead time is constant. Second, the lead time is the time between placing an order and receiving the ordered goods. Figure 5–1 clarifies

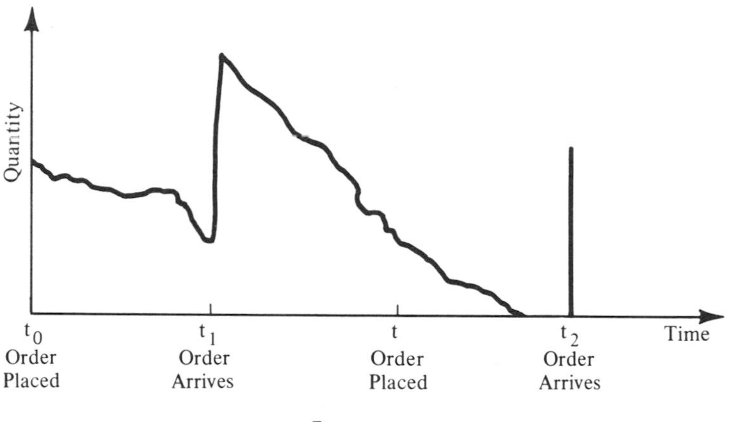

Figure 5–1

these concepts. The constant period $(t_0 - t_1)$ or $(t - t_2)$ is the lead time. The inventory cycle is defined by the interval $(t_1 - t_2)$ or $(t_0 - t)$.

Consider this case: We have already determined the optimal lot size to cover the expected demand for a given period, the length of which is the sum of the inventory cycle and the lead time. In Figure 5–1, the initial order placed would *take into account* the expected demand covering the period $(t_0 - t_2)$. (Note that we are not yet determining the *size* of the order.) This order would have to cover not only the demand during the current lead time but also the demand during the lead time immediately following, because no matter what happens we will not be receiving any additional stock before time t_2. Similarly, the safety stock to cover a random spurt in demand will cover this entire period given by $(t_0 - t_2)$ because we will not review our inventory situation before time t and will not have additional stock before time t_2. Note that, as was shown earlier, under the fixed-order system our safety stock would be just large enough to meet a reasonable spurt in demand *during the lead time alone*.

Suppose that the expected usage (normally distributed) during an inventory cycle is given by the quantity $\overline{D}_t$, and that the expected demand during the lead time is given by $\overline{D}_L$. If the corresponding standard deviations during the cycle and the lead time are σ_t and σ_L respectively, and the tolerable stockout number requires safety stock given by k times the standard deviation of demand during the relevant period, then the *maximum* quantity, M, that we should order is given by

$$M = \overline{D}_t + \overline{D}_L + k(\sigma_t + \sigma_L) \tag{11}$$

If the stock on hand at the time of placing the order is I, then the size of the order, P, is

$$P = M - I \tag{12}$$

The quantity P here is not the same as Q, defined earlier. In the first place, P does not have to be constant; as a matter of fact, it may reflect variable demand. Second, even when we assume a constant rate of demand during the planning period, the quantity on hand will vary, and the order size will reflect these variations.

It should be noted here that the derivation of M and the associated decision rule with respect to P are based upon the following simplifying assumptions:

1. We determine the length of the inventory cycle, as if the *expected* demand were the deterministic demand in the basic model of Chapter 4.
2. There are no quantity discounts. Thus the cost of acquisition per unit remains constant irrespective of the size of the order.
3. The cost of reviewing the inventory situation is lumped together with the cost of placing an order, s.

So far we have ignored the interactions between the length of the inventory cycle and the safety stock. Notice that this limitation is more crucial here than under the fixed-order system because the safety-stock level depends directly upon (among other things) the length of the cycle, as is evidenced by the term σ_t, the standard deviation of demand during the cycle.

B. Joint Determination of Safety Stock and Length of Cycle

We now turn to the problem of jointly determining the length of the inventory cycle and the safety stock.

We will still retain the assumptions of a constant lead time, an absence of quantity discounts, and the absorption of the cost of review in the cost of placing an order. We will also assume that the expected size of the order, P, remains constant throughout the planning period.

Let the planning period be T time units long (the unit may be a month, a week, or even a day). Suppose that the interval between two consecutive reviews is t units long, where t is an unknown to be determined. Then the number of orders will be given by the quantity T/t, and the total ordering cost will be

$$\$s \cdot \frac{T}{t}$$

Now each time we have an order, we want to make the sum of the quantity on hand and the quantity to be ordered equal to the (still unknown) quantity M. By the time we receive the quantity ordered, the lead-time demand would have, on the average, reduced the quantity on hand by the amount $\overline{D}_L$, the average lead-time demand. Thus we start the cycle with the total amount of

$$M - \overline{D}_L$$

units in stock.

The demand during the cycle will further reduce this stock by $\overline{D}_t$ units. This concept is shown in Figure 5–2. The length of the cycle is

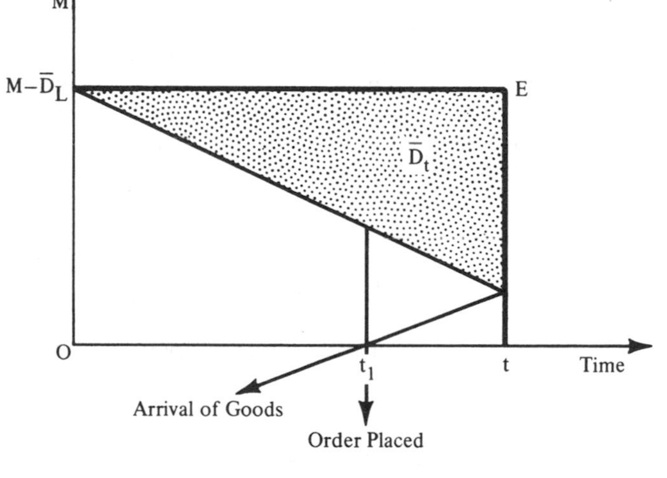

Figure 5–2

t units. Thus, if we did not have any demand, the total inventory during the cycle would have been $(M - \overline{D}_L)t$, the area represented by the rectangle $(M - \overline{D}_L)Ot\,E$ in Figure 5–2. This total inventory will be reduced by the amount $\frac{1}{2}\,\overline{D}_t t$, the shaded triangular area, because we have a demand of $\overline{D}_t$ units during the cycle. Then the average inventory will be given by

$$\frac{1}{t}\left[(M - \overline{D}_L)t - \overline{D}_t t/2\right]$$

i.e.,

$$(M - \overline{D}_L) - \frac{1}{2}\overline{D}_t$$

Since this is an average amount during a single cycle, it will still remain an average amount during the entire planning period. The average inventory in dollar terms will be

$$\$p\left[M - \frac{1}{2}\overline{D}_t - \overline{D}_L\right] \tag{13}$$

and the total inventory investment cost will be

$$\$ip\left[M - \frac{1}{2}\overline{D}_t - \overline{D}_L\right] \tag{14}$$

We have so far derived two components of the total-cost function, the ordering cost and the inventory investment cost. The last component of the total-cost function is the stockout or back-order cost. If demand during any cycle is characterized by a random variable x, the probability of this demand may be described by $f(x)$. In order that we incur the back-order cost, the random demand x should be in excess of the maximum stock level, M. Thus the expected stockout quantity during an inventory cycle will be

$$G(M) = \int_M^\infty (x - M)f(x)\,dx \tag{15}$$

Since there are T/t cycles during the planning period, the total stockout, on the average, will be

$$T/t \int_M^\infty (x - M)f(x)\,dx \tag{15'}$$

Since the cost per unit of stockout is $\$u$, the total stockout cost will be

$$\$u \cdot T/t\left[\int_M^\infty (x - M)f(x)\,dx\right] \tag{16}$$

Thus, the total-cost function will be

Total cost = order cost + investment cost + stockout cost

$$Tc = s \cdot T/t + ip\left(M - \frac{1}{2}\overline{D}_t - \overline{D}_L\right) + u \cdot T/t\left[\int_M^\infty (x - M)f(x)\,dx\right] \quad (17)$$

There are two unknown variables, t and M. Minimization of the total cost requires (1) partial differentiation of Tc with respect to t and M, (2) setting the resultant expressions equal to 0, and (3) resolving these two simultaneous equations. Thus:

$$\frac{\partial Tc}{\partial t} = 0 = \frac{-sT}{t^2} - \frac{ip}{2}\frac{\partial(\overline{D}_t)}{\partial t} - \frac{uT}{t^2}\int_M^\infty (x - M)f(x)\,dx \quad (18)$$

$$\frac{\partial Tc}{\partial M} = 0 = ip - \frac{uT}{t}\int_M^\infty f(x)\,dx \quad (19)$$

Note that $\overline{D}_t$ is an *explicit* function of t, even though our formulation does not show it. This is obvious when we see that t is composed of 1, 2, . . . , t time units; if demand per time unit is $g(x)$, then

$$\overline{D}_t = t\int xg(x)\,dx$$

Even when we define the average demand during a cycle in this fashion, we find that the resultant expressions are only implicit functions of t and M. Thus, the approach to a solution will be a trial-and-error method for different values of t. Instead of using equations (18) and (19), however, we will directly use the total-cost expression given by equation (17).

For each value of t, the unique optimal value of M will still be given by rearranging equation (19) in the following form:

$$\int_M^\infty f(x)\,dx = \frac{ipt}{uT}$$

i.e.,

$$1 - F(M) = \frac{ipt}{uT}$$

or,

$$F(M) = \frac{uT - ipt}{uT} \quad (20)$$

As a demonstration of this method of solution, let us solve the following problem.

Example:

$$T = 12 \text{ months}$$
$$\overline{D}_L = 100 \text{ units}$$
$$\overline{D} = 1{,}200 \text{ units}$$
$$p = \$100$$
$$i = .10$$
$$u = \$150$$
$$s = \$1{,}000$$
$$\sigma = 20 \text{ units (standard deviation for the lead time)}$$

Note that this example is the same as that given on page 109. We will assume, for simplicity, that demand is normally distributed.

1. We start with Q (basic) = 490 units. In that case

$$t = Q/\left(\frac{D}{T}\right) = 4.9 \text{ months}$$

Since the lead time is 1 month,

$$\overline{D}_1 = (\overline{D}_t + \overline{D}_L) = 590 \text{ units}$$

Similarly,

$$\sigma_1 = \sigma(t + L)^{1/2} = 48.798$$

2. Now

$$F\left(\frac{M - \overline{D}_1}{\sigma_1}\right) = \left(\frac{uT - ipt}{uT}\right) = .972778$$

From the normal distribution tables, we find that

$$\frac{M - \overline{D}_1}{\sigma_1} = 1.92423$$

or

$$M = 683.48 \text{ units}$$

3. The total cost will be

$$Tc = s\frac{T}{t} + ip[M - \overline{D}_L - \overline{D}_t/2]$$
$$+ (uT/t)\left[\sigma_1\phi\left(\frac{M - \overline{D}_1}{\sigma_1}\right) - (M - \overline{D}_1)\frac{ipt}{uT}\right]$$
$$= \$6{,}018.42$$

[Note: the expression for the shortage cost is derived from equation (16).]

We now reduce the value of t by .05 units, and repeat the process. The resultant revelant values are given in Table 5–1.

TABLE 5–1

t	M (integrated value)	*Total Cost*
4.9 months	683 units	$6018.42
4.85	678	6015.78
4.8	673	6013.67
4.75	668	6012.10
4.7	663	6011.10
4.65	657	6010.68
4.6	652	6010.86
4.55	647	6011.66
4.5	642	6013.10

Thus the optimal value of t^* is 4.65 months. The corresponding value of M^* is 658 units. Since the expected demand will be 565 units $[(4.65+1$ month lead time$) \times 100]$, the safety stock will be $658 - 565 = 93$ units.

IV. Comparison of the Two Systems

The two examples that have been provided are instructive because they demonstrate the characteristics of the two systems, the fixed-order system (*FOS*) and the fixed-period system (*FPS*).

Under the *FOS*, the length of the inventory cycle will be

$$\frac{498 \times 12}{1,200} = 4.98$$

months. On the other hand, under the *FPS*, the length of the cycle is 4.65 months. Thus we find that inventory cycles are shorter under the *FPS* than under the *FOS*.

When we look at the safety-stock level, we find that under the FOS, it is 9 units. Under the *FPS*, the safety stock is $658 - 565 = 93$ units. Thus we find that the safety stock is larger and the length of the cycle is shorter under the *FPS* than under the *FOS*. As we have seen earlier, the larger safety stock under the *FPS* may be explained by the fact that the safety stock covers not only the lead time (as is the case with the *FOS* but also one whole additional inventory cycle. Since this stock is larger, the cost of inventory investment will also be higher under the *FPS*; consequently, this investment cost is offset partially by a slightly larger number of orders. Thus the inventory cycle, an inverse of the number of orders, is smaller under the *FPS*.

Does this mean that administering the *FPS* is more expensive than administering the *FOS*? Before we answer this question, we must consider some factors that affect the choice of a system.

First, we have not taken into account the costs of maintaining inventory records and making physical reviews. Under the *FPS,* we need to inspect and review our inventory situation only periodically, and this may obviate the need for accurate perpetual inventory records. These costs, what Starr and Miller call the "systematic costs,"[4] may tilt the balance in favor of the *FPS.* The current practice of computerizing the inventory system, however, would favor the *FOS* because orders are processed and inventories are updated instantaneously for many items and many locations under an efficient computerized inventory system.

Second, when inventory investment costs are high, the larger amount of safety stock required (for the same degree of customer service) under the *FPS* suggests a shortcoming of the *FPS.* High inventory investment costs may be due to a number of reasons, such as high value per unit of usage over a considerably long period of time.

Third, when ordering costs are large, and it is possible to order a number of items from one supplier (or use, say, a carload of items to be transported), it is worthwhile to consider the *FPS* system. When these items are supplied by individual suppliers, and discounts are available on purchases of separate items alone, the *FOS* may be preferred to the *FPS.*

The *FPS* decision rules show a great sensitivity to the most recent sales. Thus when there are definite trends in the usage (but these are detectable only after a long time), the *FPS* will be more effective. Note that some spurts or declines in demand may not be indicative of a trend at all. In such a case, use of the *FPS* will be particularly dangerous for a multi-level inventory system, i.e., a system where input at one level becomes output for other levels. Such situations usually involve a considerable lag of time for proper adjustment, so feedback built into the *FPS* can lead to excessive stocks or very large stockout situations.

So far we have not covered all factors (nor have we touched upon interaction among the few factors) that affect the selection of a particular system. Suffice it to say, the discussion above does indicate that a particular system is not superior to the other in all situations, and a great deal depends upon the demand, cost, and product characteristics.

V. The (s,S) System

Under the *FOS,* once we have decided upon the optimal level of service to the customers, the decision rules to be observed are as follows:

1. An order is to be placed when the inventory on hand reaches the level r.
2. The size of the order would be Q units.

[4] Starr and Miller [1962, pp. 12–13, 124].

The decision rules under the *FPS* would be:

1. Review the inventory situation at intervals of t time units.
2. Place an order of the size P (given by the difference between M and inventory on hand).

An analytical system that combines the features of these two basic systems is known as the (s,S) system. Under this system, we review our inventory situation periodically but place an order only if the inventory on hand does not exceed s units; in that case, the order size will be such as to bring the level of the inventories up to S units. If the inventory on hand does exceed s units, we will not place an order. The level of s units corresponds to the reorder level r under the FOS. At the same time, the actual order size would vary as P does in the FPS. Even though the rules under this system are easy to apply, they are extremely difficult to formulate, particularly when we deal with demand that does *not* have an exponential distribution.[5] Moreover, "the exponential distribution is seldom a realistic representation of the density for the demand in a period . . . [thus] the result . . . obtained does not seem to be of great practical value." [6] For these reasons, we shall not deal with the analytical formulation of the (s,S) policy. However, it is possible to choose among the given (s,S)-policy alternatives under the assumption of discrete demand distribution. We shall undertake that task now.

* Uncertainty and the Markov Process

When discrete demand distribution is a reasonable assumption, and it is appropriate to assume that the influence of past periods on the present is solely contained in the previous period, we can rely upon the Markov process (described in Chapter 2) for determining inventory policy. As before, it should be noted that this procedure will not provide us with an analytical solution; instead, it will enable us to choose the "best" among the alternatives considered.

Suppose we are considering a policy of periodic inventory review. According to one policy alternative, we order Q_i units if the inventory on hand, i, does not exceed r units. The value of Q_i is given by

$$Q_i = M - i, \qquad i \leq r$$

$$Q_i = 0, \qquad i > r$$

Here, both M and r are predetermined values for an alternative.

For simplicity, we shall make the following assumptions:

---

[5] cf. Hadley & Whitin [1963, p. 277].

[6] *ibid.*, p. 280.

1. The lead time, l units, is a known constant smaller than the inventory cycle, t units.
2. Orders are backlogged during the lead time; but they become lost sales if they remain unfulfilled beyond one inventory cycle (during which they arrived).
3. There is no cost for orders backlogged during the lead times; however, the lost-sales cost is $\$u$ per unit.
4. $\$c$ is the inventory investment cost *per unit per cycle.*
5. The demand distribution is known, and it remains constant for each inventory cycle.

Let us define the level of inventories as "states." Because the level of inventories, by definition, cannot exceed the value M, the largest state will be M. However, inventories can be negative—e.g., when orders are not fulfilled. For convenience, we will assume that the largest negative value possible for inventories is $-a$ $(a > 0)$. Thus, for our problem, we will have $(M + a)$ states to consider.

Suppose that for a particular inventory cycle the initial stock is i units $(i > r)$. We will not place an order because $i > r$. Now the ending stock will be exactly i units if there is no demand during the inventory cycle under consideration. If the probability of demand for k units is given by p_k, then the transition probability, p_{ii} (as defined in Chapter 2), will be given by

$$p_{ii} = p_0, \qquad i > r$$

$$p_{ij} = p_{(i-j)}, \qquad i > r$$

and

$$p_{ij} = p_{(M-j)}, \qquad i \leq r$$

Thus the knowledge of the demand distribution enables us to construct the transition matrix.

Now, just as we had the "payment matrix" for collection of accounts receivable,[7] we will need the "cost matrix" for the inventory system. This matrix would contain elements that represent costs corresponding to the elements of the transition matrix. In particular, these elements are the costs associated with the transition of the system for the ith state to the jth state. We will consider four alternatives:

1. $i > r$, and $j \geq 0$
2. $i > r$, and $j < 0$
3. $i \leq r$, and $j \geq 0$
4. $i \leq r$, and $j < 0$

Alternatives 3 and 4 will have the order cost, whereas alternatives 1 and 2 will not contain any order cost. Similarly, alternatives 2 and 4

[7] See Chapter 2, pp. 38–39.

will have the lost-sales cost given by $(-\$ju)$, whereas alternatives 1 and 3 will not have any lost-sales cost.

Consideration of the inventory investment cost can be facilitated by examining Figure 5–3.

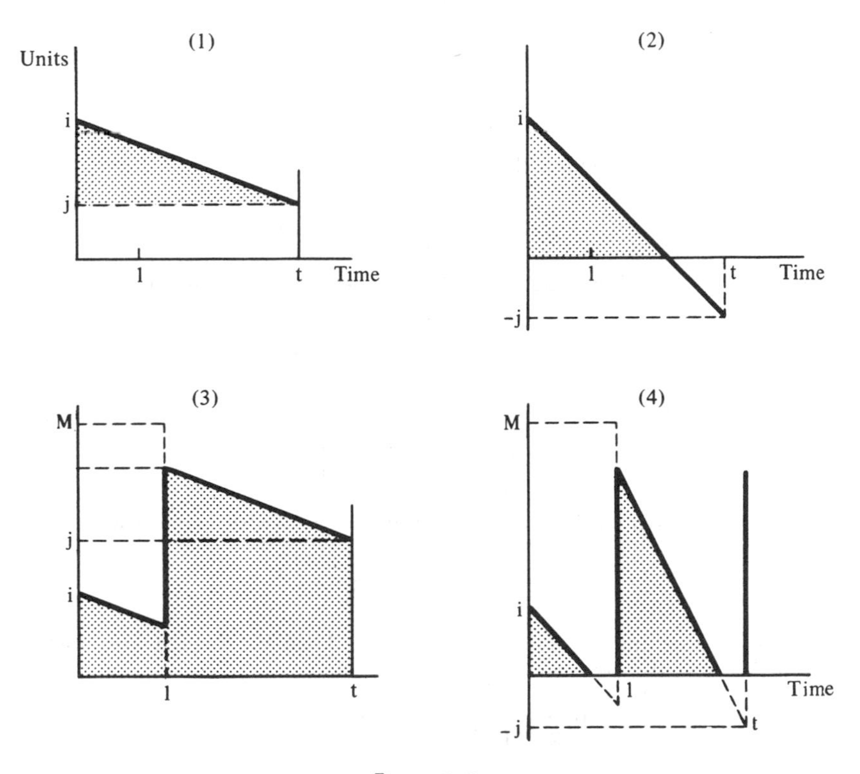

Figure 5–3

The shaded area represents the total inventory during a cycle. The average inventory will be given by

$$\frac{1}{t} \text{ (shaded area)}$$

1. When $i > r$, $j \geq 0$, the shaded area is

$$\frac{(i + j)t}{2}$$

2. When $i > r$, $j < 0$, the shaded area is a triangle whose base is not known. However, our assumption of a uniform rate of demand is helpful. The total demand during the period is $(i - j)$. (Note: $j < 0$.) Thus the rate of demand

will be $\frac{(i-j)}{t}$. The inventory of i units depletes at this rate, so the number of time units in which i units are depleted will be

$$\frac{i \cdot t}{(i-j)}$$

Consequently, the shaded area is

$$\frac{1}{2} \cdot i \cdot \frac{i \cdot t}{(i-j)}$$

3. When $i \leq r$, $j > 0$, again, the demand rate will be

$$\frac{(M-j)}{t}$$

per unit of time. Thus, at the end of the lead time, inventories will be

$$i - \frac{l(M-j)}{t}$$

units. Then the inventory during the lead time will be

$$\frac{1}{2}\left[2il - l^2 \frac{(M-j)}{t}\right]$$

In the remainder of the inventory cycle, we start with inventories of

$$M - i + i - \frac{l(M-j)}{t} = M - \frac{l(M-j)}{t}$$

units. The ending inventories are j units. Then the shaded area for the remainder of the cycle will be

$$\frac{(t-l)}{2}\left[M - \frac{l(M-j)}{t} + j\right].$$

Thus the total shaded area will be equal to

$$\frac{1}{2}\left[2il - l^2 \frac{(M-j)}{t}\right] + \left(t - \frac{l}{2}\right)\left[M\left(1 - \frac{l}{t}\right) + j\left(1 + \frac{l}{t}\right)\right].$$

4. When $i \leq r$, $j < 0$, the demand rate during the cycle will be

$$d = \frac{(M-j)}{t}$$

per time unit. During the lead time, inventories of i units will last i/d time units. Thus the shaded area during the first phase of the cycle will be

$$\frac{i}{2} \cdot \frac{i}{d} = \frac{i^2 t}{2(M-j)}$$

Now, upon receipt of the ordered goods, the back orders from the lead time will be fulfilled, and the inventories will be (M-dl) units. This stock will last $\left(\frac{M - dl}{d}\right)$ time units. Thus the shaded area for the second phase will be given by

$$\frac{(M - dl)^2}{2d}$$

i.e.,

$$\frac{t}{2(M - j)}\left[M - l\,\frac{(M - j)}{t}\right]^2$$

The total shaded area will now be

$$\frac{t}{2(M - j)}\left[i^2 + \left\{M - l\,\frac{(M - j)}{t}\right\}^2\right]$$

The average inventory investment cost under each alternative will be found by:

$$\$\,\frac{c}{t}\,(\text{the shaded area})$$

If the discount rate is k, and $v = (1 - k)^{-1}$, then the total discounted inventory cost, $V_i(t)$, for an initial stock of i units and for the planning horizons of t inventory cycles will be as follows:

$$V_i(t) = \sum_j p_{ij}[c_{ij} + vV_j(t - 1)]$$

For a very large value of t, we get[8]

$$V_i = \sum_j \sum_k n_{ij}m_{jk}$$

where $$[N] = [I - vP]^{-1}$$

and $$m_{jk} = p_{jk}c_{jk}$$

Because our initial inventory level is i, it seems reasonable to compute V_i for each of the policy alternatives and select the one with the minimum cost, V_i^*.

However, one nagging question remains. It is only by chance that our *initial* stock is i units; it might well have been $(i + 1)$ or $(i + 2)$ units. Would the "optimal" solution have been the same for different *initial* stock levels? Not necessarily. Fortunately, we can use the results we have derived so far to come up with a more accurate answer.

---

[8] For a proof, see pp. 45–46.

Our basic cost equation is

$$V_i(t) = \sum_j m_{ij} + v \sum_j p_{ij} V_j(t-1)$$

For a large value of t, we have

$$V_i = \sum_j m_{ij} + v \sum_j p_{ij} V_j \tag{21}$$

We shall use equation (21) for the iterative process[9] of finding the optimal alternative from among the available alternatives.

1. Suppose that we have two alternatives, A and B, and three states. In that case, we will compute

$$V_1^A = \sum_j m_{1j}^A + v \sum_j p_{1j}^A V_j^A$$

Similarly, we will find the values V_2^A, V_3^A, V_1^B, V_2^B, and V_3^B. On the basis of these values, we find that

$$V_1^A < V_1^B$$
$$V_2^A > V_2^B$$
$$V_3^A > V_3^B$$

2. Now, we create a *new* policy composed of the inventory policy associated with alternative A for $i = 1$ and with alternative B for $i = 2,3$. Let us define this new policy as alternative C. Then we will compute

$$V_i^C = \sum_j m_{ij}^C + v \sum_j p_{ij}^C V_j^C \tag{22}$$

where the transition and payment matrices associated with alternative C have the first row from alternative A and the other two rows from alternative B. Similarly, V_j^C on the *right side of* equation (22) is given by V_1^A, V_2^B, V_3^B for $j = 1$, 2, and 3 respectively.
3. We will now compare the value V_1^C, V_2^C, and V_3^C computed in step (2) with V_1^A, V_2^B, and V_3^B from step (1). If the new policy is decidedly better for *all three* states, we have found that alternative C is the optimal one; otherwise, we will create a new alternative, D, and repeat the process as suggested in step (2) with proper modifications.

VI. Control of Multi-item Inventories

A. Selection of Items for Evaluation

As was noted in Chapter 4, the financial manager is not directly in charge of inventory management, especially in large firms. When there

[9] The description of the iterative procedure is based upon Howard [1960, Chapter 7].

is a large number of items, he naturally cannot look into every item to ascertain the efficiency of the inventory system. The question is what items deserve his attention and scrutiny.

As a starting point, it is clear that the "*A, B, C*" system[10] of classifying items; that is, classifying items into three groups according to their usage, should be still helpful for selecting important items. However, the financial manager cannot rely exclusively on this system because safety stocks play a significant role in inventory systems under uncertainty. To see why this is so, let us first examine the relationship between the shortage-cost coefficient, u, and the safety stock. Under the *FOS*, equation (8) can be written in the following form:

$$1 - F(r) = \frac{ip}{uN} \tag{23}$$

where ip = inventory investment cost per unit per planning period

N = the number of orders in the planning period

r = the reorder point

$F(r)$ = probability that demand will not exceed r units

Thus, the larger the value of u, the smaller the value of $[1 - F(r)]$, and, consequently, the larger the value of $F(r)$. For a given demand distribution, a large $F(r)$ is directly related to a large value of r. Now the reorder point is defined as

$$r = \overline{D}_L + k\sigma_L$$

where $\overline{D}_L$ = expected demand during the lead time

$k\sigma_L$ = the safety stock ($k \geq 0$)

σ_L = the standard deviation of demand for the lead time

Thus, it follows that a large value of u leads to a large amount of safety stock, and vice versa. For a given demand distribution, a large value of u implies a large value of k—a surrogate for "satisfaction of customers' needs." On the other hand, when *only* the value of k is given for all items, items with large standard deviations will have a comparatively large safety stock, and thereby a large *imputed* value for u.

When we examine the total-cost equation for the *FOS*, equation (5),

[10] See Chapter 4, pp. 99–100.

it is obvious that a relatively large safety stock would imply a large amount of inventory investment cost. Thus, for an acceptable level of stockout, *k*, items with greater fluctuations in usage (i.e., a large σ_L) will have a much larger imputed shortage cost, *u*, and total inventory investment cost. Often items that have low usage tend to have wider fluctuations in demand. Even if these items have a high price tag, their expected usage in terms of dollars may be still low—low enough so that we may classify them in category *B* or *C*.

If these items with low usage, high price, and a large variance were stocked with the same level of acceptable stockout, *k*, that applied to high-usage, low-price, and low-variance items, the safety stock and the *total* cost for the inventory system will be comparatively much larger. In that case, it is worthwhile for the financial manager to scrutinize the former category of items (low usage, high price, and large variance) even when the "*A, B, C*" system dictates against this practice because of the low usage.

Although we have been referring to the *FOS* system in the preceding discussion above, the reasoning does not change for the *FPS*; as a matter of fact, the safety-stock level is much larger under this system than under the FOS, and therefore more important in economic terms.

This implication for the inventory system with respect to low-usage, high-price, and high-variance items and their safety stock is not so startling as it sounds. As a matter of fact, the spare-parts inventory of discontinued models, for instance, shows that managers are aware of this implication. Because the demand for such spare parts is often erratic and highly unpredictable, the manager decides to keep low inventories of these items in spite of the fact that he faces an excessive production (or procurement) cost in case of shortage.

B. Relevant Indices and Their Construction

So far, we have been examining the question of which items deserve the financial manager's scrutiny. We now address ourselves to the question of what indices enable the manager to evaluate the system effectively.

Inventory systems are based upon three types of cost: ordering cost, investment cost, and shortage cost. The indices employed for system evaluation should, accordingly, be related in some way to these cost measures. Basically, we can divide the indices into two categories: "stock" measures and "flow" measures. Flow measures span a predefined period. Stock measures provide the status of an index at the *end* of the relevant period. For instance, the number of orders placed is related to a specific period and thus is a flow measure; the number of orders placed but outstanding (during the lead time) is related to a specific instant in time and thus is a stock measure. Needless to say, a variety of indices are possible; here, however, we shall confine our attention to three of the basic indices:

1. Frequency of orders
2. Average inventories (dollar value)
3. Expected back order or lost sales (in physical units)

It should be noted that point estimates of indices such as those listed above are rarely useful. Instead, their ranges (say, based on variance of the index number) are preferred. For convenience, we shall deal only with the *expected value* of these indices.[11]

For the *FOS,* it follows from equations (3) and (4) that knowledge of N^* and r^* enables us to find the frequency of orders (N^*), average inventories ($\overline{D}/2N^* + r^* - \overline{D}_L$), and the expected back orders [$N^* \cdot G(r)$]. Similarly, for the FPS, knowledge of the decision variables t^* and M^* provides us with the frequency of orders (T/t^*), average inventories [equation (13)], and the expected shortages [equation (15′)].

For the (s,S) system in the framework of the Markov process, the task is somewhat more complex than for the two systems described above. Here we have to find the steady-state (or limiting) probabilities α_i so that the inventory level will be i units for a given item at the beginning of a particular inventory cycle. Recall that we have $(M + a)$ possible values, where a states represent "negative" values of inventories. Now, if (α) represents a row-vector of steady-state probabilities, and P represents the transition matrix, then

$$\alpha P = \alpha$$

and

$$\sum_i \alpha_i = 1$$

are true by definition: if the system is in equilibrium, one more inventory cycle will not change the steady-state probabilities; similarly, the sum of steady-state probabilities for all possible values of i is 1. This set of equations provides the unique solution of the steady-state probabilities.

Suppose that our inventory level at the beginning of the cycle is i units ($i \leq r$). For all such values of $i \leq r$, we will place orders. Thus the probability of placing an order during a cycle is

$$\sum_{i=-a}^{r} \alpha_i$$

[11] The issue of ranges directly leads us to the problem of index probability distribution. Since indices are based upon multi-items, the desired probability distribution is formed through a convolution of distributions of relevant products. Because the expected value notion, particularly under the independence assumption, does not require such convolutions, we confine ourselves to only the expected value of indices.

We have (T/t) cycles during the relevant planning period, so the number of orders placed will be given by

$$T/t \sum_{i=-a}^{r} \alpha_i$$

Because the beginning of a cycle also represents the end of the previous cycle, $(i)\alpha_i$, for non-negative values of i, represents the average physical inventories. Thus the average ending inventories (physical units) will be

$$\sum_{i=0}^{M} i\alpha_i \tag{24}$$

When the value of i is negative at the beginning of a cycle, it represents lost sales of i units during the previous cycle. Then

$$\sum_{i=-a}^{-1} i\alpha_i \tag{25}$$

represents the expected value of lost sales (in physical units) during a cycle, and

$$-\left(\frac{T}{t}\right) \sum_{i=-a}^{-1} i\alpha_i \tag{26}$$

will represent the expected lost sales (physical units) during the planning period.

Other indices of interest can be readily devised through simple manipulations. For example, we noted that the probability of placing an order is α_i, and the average size of the order will be

$$\sum_{i=-a}^{r} (S - i)\alpha_i \tag{27}$$

So far we have derived indices for only one product. When we have a multi-item inventory, we can derive these indices for each of the products; but we are not so much interested in management of *each* of these products as we are in the *aggregate* measures. For this purpose, all items are stated in a homogeneous measure for the purpose of constructing the indices. One such measure, and this is the measure of greatest interest to the financial manager, is the monetary unit.

If we assume that demand distributions of all items (or items of interest) are independent of each other, the task of constructing indices is considerably simplified. Once we have the relevant indices for each product in physical-unit measures, we can multiply each of them with relevant unit prices.[12] Then, we have only to sum the relevant quantities for all products; for instance, once we derive a lost-sales measure in physical units for product *k*, we can multiply the measure by the unit price of product *k*. The total lost-sales cost will be given by the sum of all such products *k*.

VII. Conclusion

The examination of inventory systems under uncertainty in this chapter has shown that utilizing probabilistic demand values in place of deterministic demand has some significant implications for financial management. First, the *FOS* and the *FPS* are no longer equivalent in economic terms, as was the case under certainty. The difference arises from the role played by the safety-stock level, which is considerably larger under the *FPS* than under the *FOS*, even for the same degree of service to customers. Second, we no longer can rely exclusively on the "*A, B, C*" system to choose items worthy of attention by top management. Again, the role played by safety stocks is crucial at this juncture: if low-usage items (which will be ignored under the "*A, B, C*" system) have high variances and high price tags, the same degree of customer service can lead to a policy of excessive stockage.

Appendix

$$G(r) = \int_r^\infty (x - r)f(x)\,dx$$

or
$$G(r) = \int_r^\infty (x - \overline{D}_L + \overline{D}_L - r)N(x; \overline{D}_L, \sigma)\,dx$$

$$= \int_r^\infty (x - \overline{D}_L)N(x; \overline{D}_L, \sigma)\,dx + \int_r^\infty (\overline{D}_L - r)N(x; \overline{D}_L, \sigma)\,dx$$

$$= \sigma\int_r^\infty \left(\frac{x - \overline{D}_L}{\sigma}\right) N(x; \overline{D}_L, \sigma)\,dx + (\overline{D}_L - r)\int_r^\infty N(x; \overline{D}_L, \sigma)\,dx$$

[12] This procedure of multiplying by the relevant unit prices only creates a crude control measure, because such a measure can be easily manipulated—particularly when it deals with only one aspect at a time, such as inventories or lost sales—by lower management in such a way as to effectively conceal violations of top management policy directives; for instance, a large number of excessive purchases of low-priced items can be hidden behind under-purchase of a high-priced item. Wagner [1962, Chapter 3—especially section 3.2] suggests a more appropriate, albeit complex, procedure. We can describe the procedure briefly as follows. First, we define the total cost index under different prevailing states, such as the initial inventory value above *r*, above zero, and negative (when backorders are permitted). Second, instead of multiplying the physical quantities by the unit price, or the unit inventory cost, etc., we derive the set of *artificial* dollar values—somewhat akin to the "shadow prices" in such a way that the expected value of the control index is minimized only when the managerial policy directives are followed. This task of deriving the artificial dollar values is greatly facilitated by the Monte Carlo simulation technique. Finally, these values are attached to the relevant physical quantities and summed to derive the appropriate index number.

We have divided $G(r)$ into two parts in such a way as to facilitate transformation of the random variable in x into a *standardized normal variable.*

Let v be the standardized normal variable, i.e.,

$$v = (x - \overline{D}_L)/\sigma.$$

When $$x = r, \qquad v = (r - \overline{D}_L)/\sigma = R/\sigma.$$

Then,

$$G(r) = \sigma \int_{R/\sigma}^{\infty} vN(v)\, dv + (\overline{D}_L - r) \int_{R/\sigma}^{\infty} N(v)\, dv$$

$$= \sigma\ \overline{2\Pi}\ e^{-\left(\frac{r-\overline{D}_L}{\sigma}\right)^2/2} + (\overline{D}_L - r)\left[1 - F\left(\frac{r - \overline{D}_L}{\sigma}\right)\right]$$

$$= \sigma\phi\left(\frac{r - \overline{D}_L}{\sigma}\right) + (\overline{D}_L - r)\left[1 - F\left(\frac{r - \overline{D}_L}{\sigma}\right)\right]$$

Part Three

CASH MANAGEMENT

THE level of cash balance in a firm is affected by a variety of transactions, and the *degree of control* exercised by the decision maker varies for different types of transactions. The existing literature on cash management perceives controllable transactions at three levels. At the first level, only transactions dealing with marketable securities are regarded as controllable. In this case, the relevant literature treats cash balance as a problem in either inventory management or portfolio management. If cash balance is considered a problem in inventory management, cash is considered a *physical* asset that facilitates the synchronization of transactions; thus *net* cash flows are treated as uncontrollable variables like sales (or demand) in inventory management. If cash balance is considered a problem in portfolio management, cash is a *financial* asset and cash balances are determined in the light of risk-return characteristics of other financial assets or securities. In Chapter 6, we will deal with cash from both these viewpoints. The treatment of cash at this stage is consistent with our treatment of accounts receivable and inventories, which hitherto have also been considered without any direct consideration of other asset forms.

At the *second* level, cash is dealt with in conjunction not only with marketable securities but also with other forms of current assets and current liabilities. In this sense, cash serves as a pivotal point for integrating management of working-capital components. Of course, controllable transactions affecting (and affected by) cash balances increase in complexity; and conventional analytic frameworks capable of yielding generalized insights through optimization cannot handle these complexities without a great deal of abstraction. In Chapter 7, it is shown that cash as an integrating force can best be handled in programming frameworks in order to provide optimal, numerical solutions in certain situations (under certainty as well as uncertainty)—not only because this approach is convenient but also because programming frameworks are flexible and robust in handling a wide variety of situations.

At the *third* level, cash is considered a residual form of asset. Cash management covers decisions encompassing not only routine activities involving working capital but also nonroutine transactions of capital budgeting and changes in the capital structure. At this point, the element of uncertainty over time is added to the increased complexity; hence, even programming techniques become awkward in handling these relationships. In Chapter 8, we will examine cash in this broad perspective by means of the framework of simulation, which allows the manager a glimpse of the probable impact of these complex relationships without any assurance for formulating optimal cash management policies.

It is clear from the above description that, apart from controllability, we can also classify transactions affecting cash balances on two other dimensions: (1) their degree of predictability and (2) their frequency within the planning period—or their routine or nonroutine nature. Two characteristics of these different dimensions are worth noting. First, these dimensions are neither independent nor totally related. Second, the degree of importance attached to them varies in different situations. Consequently, we cannot construct a *general* model useful for all situations; we will, instead, deal with a variety of models suggested in the literature and stress their ranking of these dimensions, or means of classification, in order to bring out their effectiveness in particular situations.

6

Cash Management and Marketable Securities

I. Introduction

Traditionally, cash management has meant little more than maintaining sufficient cash balances to meet current obligations. Thus the financial officer in charge of cash management regards the timing and size of all transactions affecting cash balances as uncontrollable. The only exception to this is the sale or purchase of marketable securities. If the financial manager regards cash balances as excessive, he siphons off the excess cash balance by purchasing securities; on the other hand, if a cash shortage is imminent, he augments cash balances through the sale of securities. The descriptive literature on this subject does of course consider important practical alternatives to the sale and purchase of securities, such as postponement and prepayment of obligations; but by and large such alternatives are rarely regarded as an integral part of the planning process.

Suppose that, for a given planning period, we are given all transactions (other than the sale and purchase of marketable securities) affecting cash balances. Effective cash management would then require consideration of the following questions:

1. What is an "adequate" cash balance that meets all obligations when they are due?

2. If cash balances are in excess of the adequate level at some point in time, is it worthwhile to invest a part (or all) of this excess in marketable securities? If so, for how long should the investment in securities be made, and what kinds of securities should be purchased?
3. If cash falls short of expected obligations, what amount of marketable securities should be sold, and when?

At this point, it is necessary to draw a distinction between cash and marketable securities. Cash is "any asset that is widely and legally used as an exchange medium." [1] Cash is a benchmark for liquidity. All other assets have less liquidity than cash in the sense that their transformation into cash requires time, expense, or both. Marketable securities are deemed less liquid than cash because they can normally be disposed of instantaneously, but their conversion into cash requires some transaction costs. However, this relative illiquidity of investment in marketable securities—requiring postponement of consumption—has a reward (the expected rate of return) that the holder of cash has to forego. From these considerations, it is obvious that cash management involves costs not unlike those connected with inventory management. Inventory models, therefore, seem to be applicable to cash and capable of resolving issues such as what amount of liquid assets should be held in the forms of cash and marketable securities, and what amount of securities should be sold at what point in time. In the first part of this chapter, we will devote attention to these issues from the viewpoint of inventory management.

In the marketplace, there are different types of marketable securities. They differ in terms of their maturity, promised rates of return and, in general, risk characteristics. For instance, "current" government obligations (maturing in less than a year) differ in maturity. Even though the return of the principal and interest is certain for these obligations upon maturity, they involve different amounts of risk as regards the need to liquidate them *before* maturity: movements in interest rate affect the prices of these various fixed-obligation securities differently. This characteristic has two implications for cash management. First we cannot consider marketable securities as a bundle of homogeneous securities; we must, then, consider the proportion of investment in different types of securities. Second, and perhaps more important, ordinarily we cannot consider only the expected return for a security; we must also evaluate its risk potential. Portfolio-management theory considers the issue of determining cash balances in the light of availability of different securities embodying different risk-return characteristics. We will describe the basic outline of portfolio-management theory in the second part of this chapter.

We can conclude from our analysis that the inventory-theory approach and the portfolio-theory approach are complementary rather than mutually exclusive. Inventory theory neglects (or is awkward in

---

[1] D. Orr [1970], p. 8.

handling) the availability of different securities; portfolio theory fails to accommodate the basic reason for holding cash, i.e., liquidity needs, because it assumes that all risky securities are liquidated only at the *end* of the period and that the interim need for cash will be either adequately satisfied by the optimal cash balance or postponed until the end of the period.

II. Cash Management and Inventory Theory

A. Cash Balances and the EOQ Model

In this chapter, cash and marketable securities are the two alternative asset forms under consideration. Cash provides the liquidity needed to fulfill future obligations that are not perfectly synchronized with future inflow. Marketable securities provide a return on investment of idle cash. Hence, if we are to treat the cash-balance problem in the framework of inventory theory,

1. The *setup cost* will be the cost of converting the securities into cash.
2. The *carrying cost* will be the opportunity cost of holding cash, given by the return on marketable securities.

For deterministic flows, the simplicity of the *EOQ* model described in Chapter 4 has attracted a number of authors (e.g., Baumol [1952], Bierman and McAdams [1962], Whalen [1968], and Sastry [1970]). Baumol as well as Bierman and McAdams applied the *EOQ* model in a straightforward manner; Whalen and Sastry, however, were interested in modifying the model when cash inflows result from both the sale of securities and from external borrowings.

As an approach to cash management, the *EOQ* model is less than satisfactory for a number of reasons. Before we examine these reasons, one misconception should be cleared up. Sprenkle [1967] and Resek [1967] argue that when risk is superimposed upon the deterministic *EOQ* model, there is a strange result: the precautionary balance turns out to be negative. If this were true, and the underlying causes were reasonable or widely encountered, the usefulness of the *EOQ* model for cash management would be seriously impaired. But as it turns out, their works contain two critical implicit assumptions: zero lead time and a deterministic rate of return on marketable securities that remains unaffected (i.e., there are no *additional* setup costs) even when a cash shortage does occur. As we have noted in Chapter 5, when these assumptions hold, there is no incentive for holding any safety stock.[2]

[2] cf. p. 102. Note that zero lead time in itself is a sufficient condition but not a necessary condition for nonpositive safety stock. A slight reinterpretation of Sastry's model, for example, supports this conclusion. Sastry decomposes the cash cycle of t time units into two parts: t_1 (when demand for cash is immediately met) and t_2 (when obligations are accumulated and paid at the end of the cash cycle). Thus t_2

As regards the limitations of the *EOQ* model, it is the assumptions about cash flows that create problems. We can characterize cash flows as follows: cash receipts are only periodic and result from liquidation of securities, whereas *net* cash outflows occur at a constant rate. A more precise way to describe the behavior of cash inflows is this: receipts are received *at the beginning of the planning period* and are immediately converted *without cost* into income-earning securities, which are periodically liquidated at some fixed cost. Only in this way can we avoid the issue of the transaction cost of *acquiring* securities. But, unlike the case of physical stocks, this is an unusually restrictive assumption about cash-flow behavior, particularly cash *in*flows, because not only will receipts typically be interspersed with payments but also in some cases receipts at any time t may *exceed* cash outflows resulting from payment obligations. As a result, "the cash balance can move . . . in either direction, whereas in the usual inventory model 'demand' during any period is assumed to be non-negative";[3] therefore, the physical inventory moves in only one direction during a cycle. This difficulty is accentuated when we superimpose the assumption of uncertainty. In the conventional *EOQ* model, it is assumed that production (inflows) is nonrandom and controllable, whereas sales (outflows) are random and uncontrollable. We cannot, however, characterize cash flows in this fashion, because control over inflows (or outflows) is far from absolute in most cases. One implication of this lack of control and the resulting randomness of flows is that a joint, convoluted distribution of inflows and outflows is necessary for applying an inventory-theoretic approach. Fortunately, we can avoid such a complex approach by adopting the Miller–Orr [1966] model.

B. Cash Balances and Inventory Theory under Uncertainty

Miller and Orr start with the assumption that only two forms of assets exist: cash and marketable securities. Their model, unlike the

---

time units are the lead-time period during which the firm considers it worthwhile to incur the shortage cost. This shortage cost is C_2 per dollar per unit of time. If i is the interest cost, A is the demand for the planning period T, and C_1 is the setup cost, then the average balance Q^* will be

$$\left(\frac{AC_1}{2Ti}\right)^{1/2}\left(\frac{C_2}{i+C_2}\right)\left(\frac{C_2}{i+C_2}\right)^{1/2}$$

Under the *EOQ* model, the corresponding average balance will be

$$\left(\frac{AC_1}{2Ti}\right)^{1/2}$$

Because $\left(\frac{C_2}{i+C_2}\right)\left(\frac{C_2}{i+C_2}\right)^{1/2} < 1$, Q^* will be smaller than the corresponding *EOQ* average balance—the negative difference being the negative "safety" balance under a finite lead time, when the shortage cost is finite and proportional (i.e., borrowing does not entail any setup cost).

[3] Eppen and Fama [1969], p. 121.

EOQ model, allows for cash-balance movement in both positive and negative directions: i.e., transactions can increase as well as decrease cash balances. A variety of subordinate assumptions are possible with respect to the probability of a transaction and its size. For simplicity, Miller and Orr assume that the probability is p that a transaction will *increase* the cash balance by 1 unit and q that it will *decrease* the balance by 1 unit. Transactions are assumed to be of 1 unit each.[4] In order to simplify the analysis further, they assume that

$$p = q = \frac{1}{2}$$

Because cash balances may move up and down, the questions are: What is the ideal level (or levels) of cash balance, and what actions should be taken when the actual balance deviates from this ideal? Miller and Orr suggest that instead of one ideal level, there is a *range* of ideal cash balances. When the cash balance is within this range, we do not take any action; i.e., we let the balance drift in a positive or negative direction. However, when the balance reaches the *upper* limit of the range, it is reduced to a given level by the *purchasing* of marketable securities. Similarly, when the cast balance reaches the lower limit, it is replenished by the *sale* of marketable securities. In this case, our concern is with the following issues:

1. What is the upper limit of the range?
2. What is the lower limit of the range, triggering the sale of securities?
3. What amount of securities should be purchased or sold when the cash balance reaches the upper limit or the lower limit of the range?

For convenience, let us assume that the lower limit of the ideal range is 0 and that the upper limit, h, is still to be determined. Suppose further that cash balances are brought to the level z, through the sale or purchase of securities, as soon as one of the limits is reached. Thus, when we reach the cash balance of h units, we purchase securities worth $(h - z)$ units net of transaction costs; when the balance is 0, we sell securities to bring the cash level to z units. Finally, we assume that the lead time is zero—i.e., a transfer between cash and marketable securities is instantaneous—however, the transfer cost is s units, regardless of the size of the transaction. Note that the transfer cost corresponds to the setup cost in the conventional inventory model. This process is presented in Figure 6–1.

If $P(T)$ is the probability of transfer transactions in any *unit* period, i the carrying cost per unit per period, and $E(M)$ is the average cash balance during the period, then we would like to minimize Tc, the total cost per unit period, given by

$$Tc = sP(T) + iE(M) \tag{1}$$

[4] Miller and Orr relax this assumption later.

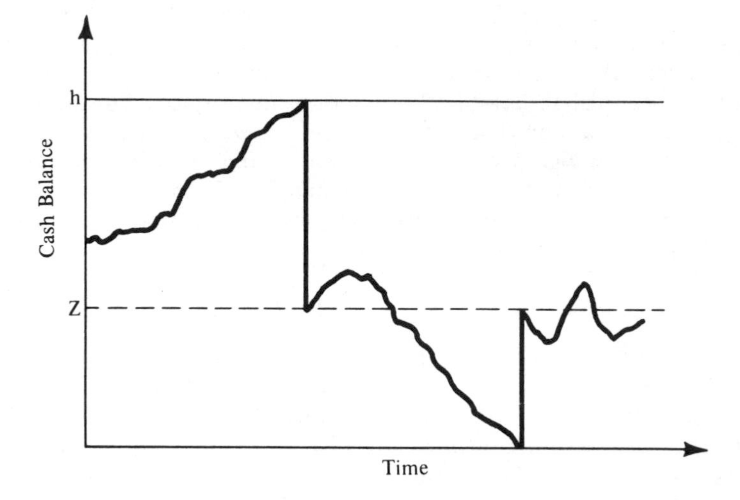

Figure 6–1. Cash-balance Movement in Miller-Orr Model

Suppose there are n uncontrollable transactions affecting cash balances. Then, under the given assumptions, as is shown in the Appendix,

$$E(M) = (h + z)/3 \tag{2}$$

and

$$P(T) = n/[z(h - z)] \tag{3}$$

Thus,

$$Tc = ns/[z(h - z)] + i(h + z)/3.$$

If we substitute $Z = (h - z)$ and partially differentiate the cost function with respect to Z and z, the optimal Z^* and z^* are derived from equating the resultant expressions with zero and simultaneously solving them. Hence,

$$z^* = \left[\frac{(3sn)}{4i}\right]^{1/3} \tag{4}$$

$$Z^* = 2z^*$$

Now, the variance of changes in cash balance for a given period is given by

$$\sigma^2 = 4npq$$

Thus, in our case, it will be

$$\sigma^2 = n$$

Then, $$z^* = \left[\frac{(3s\sigma^2)}{4i}\right]^{1/3} \tag{5}$$

and $$h^* = 3z^* \tag{6}$$

One interesting feature of this solution is that the set of decision rules is simple in spite of its somewhat complex derivation in analytical form. The set is:

1. If the cash balance falls to 0, sell securities worth z^* units.
2. If the cash balance reaches the level of $3z^*$ units, invest $2z^*$ units in securities.

The critical value z^* depends on the transfer cost and the carrying cost, as does Q^* (the optimal order size) under the conventional *EOQ* model, However, the average cash balance here, given by the quantity $E(M)$ or $4z^*/3$, depends not on the *level* (or volume) of transactions but on *uncertainty* (or variability of the size) of transactions, an intuitively appealing concept. Thus, if transactions are of uniform size and are to take place in such a way as to require minimum changes in the cash balance, naturally there will be little need for a large cash balance.

Although the set of decision rules requiring determination of values h^* and z^* in the Miller–Orr model is simple, unambiguous, and intuitively appealing, the question is to what extent underlying assumptions are crucial in deriving this (h,z) policy form. Assumptions with respect to two matters will be examined here: the transfer cost and the cash-flow characteristics.

As regards transfer costs, the assumption is that they are "purely lumpy" and symmetrical: i.e., the transaction costs are fixed and are of the same magnitude for both buying and selling securities. Eppen and Fama [1969] show that when there are only *strictly proportional transfer costs*—i.e., when cost depends on the size of the transfer—the *form* of the optimal policy would be closely related to the (h,z) policy. The only major difference is that z would be replaced by two separate numbers, z_2 and z_1. When the cash balance reaches the upper limit h, a purchase of securities should reduce it to z_2 units. If, on the other hand, the cash balance falls to 0 units,[5] a sale of securities should bring it up to z_1 units. Eppen and Fama [1968] compute numerical values of these variables for a variety of cost estimates that include fixed components of transfer cost, proportional components, or both. In general,

[5] The lower limits of 0 is associated with *infinite* shortage cost: i.e., shortages are not permitted under any circumstances. Eppen and Fama present a more general case of finite shortage cost and thus replace the lower limit 0 with D units. Their model is also more general in that they allow cash balances to move more than one unit in a period.

their study tends to support the Miller–Orr form of optimal policy under a variety of conditions.[6]

As regards cash flows, Miller and Orr assume that they are random. Randomness implies the following characteristics:

1. Stationarity. There is no persistent *trend* in cash balances. Statistically, the expected value of changes in cash balances is zero.
2. Serial independence. Today's cash outflows will not induce cash outflows (or inflows) tomorrow or at any time in the future. In statistical terms, the covariance term $COV_{t,t+i}$ between cashflow today (t) and a future period $(t + i)$ would be negligible.
3. Stability. The transactions affecting cash balances are such that there is absence of high volatility in cash balances.

In order to determine how critical these assumptions are, sensitivity analysis is necessary. Orr [1970] has derived the following conclusions from the sensitivity analysis. When there is a small (positive or negative) drift, the set of decision rules still remains stable. However, when the transfer cost is relatively large with respect to the carrying cost, a larger drift induces a more unstable optimal policy. Similarly, when serial dependence exists over a short period, the results are unstable;[7] on the other hand, cash flows inducing future flows in more distant times do not have any adverse effect on the optimal set of rules. So far as stability is concerned, one way to measure it is to devise a ratio of the optimal range $(h^* - 0)$ and σ, the standard deviation of changes. A ratio larger than the number 6 did not create any stability problem in Orr's study. In brief, the sensitivity analysis provides favorable evidence of the robustness of the Miller–Orr model under varying assumptions about changes in cash balance.[8]

Nevertheless, some nagging issues still remain. First, the assumption of homogeneous securities is questionable; among other things, different securities provide different rates of return, and the risk attached to these rates varies. Furthermore, different securities have different transfer costs, particularly with respect to liquidation. Orr has extended the analysis to three assets: cash, bonds (low-risk securities), and stocks (high-risk securities). However, he shows that the model does not per-

---

[6] Theoretically, this statement needs qualifications. Neave [1970] shows that this optimal form is less general than might be supposed from studies such as Eppen and Fama's [1968]. For instance, even when transfer costs are fixed and symmetrical, the fact that the probability function is symmetric (i.e., there are equal probabilities for increasing and decreasing the cash balance by a particular number of units) is not a *sufficient* condition for yielding a Miller–Orr form of optimal theory.

[7] We should not find this surprising because the basic premise of steady-state analysis is very likely violated when serial correlation over a relatively short period is permitted.

[8] Eppen and Fama [1968] suggest a somewhat different conclusion: that optimal policies are relatively more sensitive to the distribution of cash-balance changes than to the distribution of cost estimates.

form well in this case, if transfer costs are proportional. Furthermore, extensions to three or more assets create greater analytical complexity.

Second, the assumption of randomness has questionable implications for predictability and controllability. Randomness rules out highly predictable events such as payments on accounts payable, dividends, and taxes.[9] Moreover, the random nature of transactions implies that the financial manager—or, more properly, the cashier—can control only the sale and purchase of securities; and even this controllable activity is much more circumscribed than is apparent at first sight. Given that there are only two assets, cash and marketable securities, that are homogeneous in themselves, reshuffling of the portfolio of marketable securities (particularly in the absence of any signal from the state of cash balances) does not occur.

Finally, the assumption of randomness has one critical, uncomfortable implication for the role of marketable securities. These securities are not allowed to mature. This is possible if we assume either (1) that their maturity extends beyond the planning period (an assumption that is hard to reconcile with the concept of a steady-state analysis), *or* (2) that proceeds from maturing securities are immediately reinvested (without, presumably, incurring a transaction cost—hardly a realistic assumption). Perhaps we may rationalize this issue of maturity in one plausible way or another, but one unescapable conclusion emerges: the Miller–Orr analysis of the problem of cash balances assigns a passive role to management of marketable securities; that is, to the only activity controllable by the financial manager.

In brief, Miller and Orr provide a simple and elegant approach to cash management under uncertainty, but only by introducing uncomfortable assumptions about the random nature of cash flows and the homogeneity of marketable securities. The first assumption assigns a highly restrictive role to the maturity of securities as well as to the predictability and controllability of transactions affecting cash balances. The second assumption glosses over important issues of the portfolio effects of marketable securities. We now turn to the consideration of portfolio management that admits different securities with varying risk-return characteristics.

III. Cash Balances and Portfolio Management

As was noted above, different securities have different rates of return and varying maturities. What securities should we hold in our portfolio? For practical solutions, there are in the literature extensive discussions concerning investment objectives, characteristics of different

[9] Miller and Orr are not unaware of this uncomfortable assumption; however, they do not feel that this additional realism is desirable in face of ensuing complexity of the model, even if it were feasible to introduce it.

instruments, and specific techniques such as "riding the yield curve." [10] Analytical frameworks dealing primarily with the portfolio-theory approach have also been advanced. We will describe the essential elements of portfolio theory and investigate its applicability for cash management.

Suppose that we have N securities (or risky assets) and we want to allocate a given amount of capital (W_0) among these securities and keep a certain amount in cash. Suppose further that our planning horizon is 1 period and, as a result, we are interested in maximizing the return on our initial capital, W_0. What proportion of the initial amount should we allocate to different securities and cash? Under certainty, the problem is trivial: allocate the entire amount to the security providing the highest yield.[11] Under risk or uncertainty, the estimate of the overall rate of return would not be unique. Markowitz [1959] suggests the following approach, embodying the use of *variance* of the overall return as a measure of risk.

Let $E(r_i)$ be the expected return on the ith security, and V_i be its variance. Let x_i be the proportion of the initial amount to be invested in the ith security. Then, the overall rate of return $E(R)$ and its variance V will be provided by the following formulation:

$$E(R) = \sum_i E(r_i)x_i$$

and

$$V = \sum_i V_i x_i^2 + \sum_i \sum_{j \neq i} \text{COV}_{ij}\, x_i x_j$$

where COV_{ij} = covariance of returns between i^{th} security and j^{th} security

One characteristic of the covariance should be noted. If anticipated returns on two securities are negatively correlated, their covariance will be negative. Hence, the *combined* variance of these two securities will be smaller than the sum of their individual variances.

In order to construct the solution procedure, two critical assumptions are made. First, the capital market in which securities are traded is assumed to be perfect. Among other things, this implies that two securities with the same risk will command prices in proportion to their expected returns. Second, a typical investor has a risk-averse attitude: i.e., for a given level of risk, he will prefer a security with a higher expected rate of return to one with a lower expected rate. Similarly, for a given rate of return, he will choose a security with a lower variance over one with a higher variance. This final characteristic sug-

---

[10] For a lucid but brief treatment of these issues, see Morgan Guaranty Trust Company [1964].

[11] We will avoid here the issue of whether there can be in fact different yields under certainty.

gests a solution to the problem: maximize the expected return on the portfolio at a given level of risk. Suppose that we want the risk level to be V_0. Then, the problem is to maximize

$$E(R) = \sum_i E(r_i x_i) \tag{7}$$

subject to

$$V_0 = \sum_i V_i x_i^2 + \sum_i \sum_{j \neq i} \mathrm{COV}_{ij}\, x_i x_j \tag{8}$$

and

$$\sum_i x_i = 1 \tag{9}$$

This problem may be reformulated by using the Lagrange multipliers in the following way:

$$\text{Max } L = \sum_i E(r_i x_i) + \lambda_1 \left[V_0 - \sum_i V_i x_i^2 - \sum_i \sum_{j \neq i} \mathrm{COV}_{ij}\, x_i x_j\right] + \lambda_2 \left[1 - \sum_i x_i\right] \tag{10}$$

Setting the partial derivative of L with respect to x_i $(i = 1, 2, \ldots, N)$ equal to zero, we get

$$E(r_i) - 2\lambda_1 \left[V_i x_i + \sum_{j \neq i} \mathrm{COV}_{ij}\, x_j\right] - \lambda_2 = 0, \qquad i = 1, 2, \ldots, N \tag{11}$$

λ_1 is the shadow price associated with risk; i.e., it is the risk premium required by the investor.[12] If we invest in k $(k < N)$ securities, the risk-adjusted return forsaken on the $(k + 1)$th security will be measured by λ_2. Thus, equation (11) reflects the certainty-equivalent rate of return on the ith security.

Because $\Sigma x_i = 1$, once we determine $(N - 1)$ x_i's, the Nth variable is automatically determined. Thus we have $(N - 1)$ independent variables in x_i's that are unknown. Similarly, both λ_1 and λ_2 are unknown. But then we have N equations and $(N + 1)$ unknown variables. In order to get around this difficulty, let us prescribe the value of λ_1, and thereby solve the system of simultaneous equations given by (11). This then, will be the general solution procedure.

One characteristic of equation (11) should be noted. If the ith security is negatively correlated with other securities, then the size of the risk premium required on it will be small even when its own variance is large. This is because the sum of the terms in $[\cdot]$ will be small. This sum represents the contribution of the ith security to the overall risk of the optimal portfolio. It is obvious that this contribution will be sig-

[12] Thus a large, positive value of λ_1 signifies a high risk-aversion attitude on the part of the investor.

nificant even for a security whose own variance is small, if the sum of the covariances of the relevant security with other securities is large.

Even though we have considered above N risky securities, the analysis can be easily extended to a riskless asset, cash. Suppose we can earn r_0, the riskless interest rate, on cash. The only other difference will be that the own-variance term for cash as well as its covariances with other assets will be 0.[13] Otherwise, the analysis remains the same. Thus the portfolio analysis not only shows us how much to invest in cash as against marketable securities but also provides us with the optimal amount of investment in *each* of these securities.

It seems, then, that the problem of allocating funds among securities and cash is resolved. However, there are some operational and conceptual issues to be settled. One problem with practical implementation of the portfolio theory concerns estimation of parameters. If there are N securities, the manager has to estimate N expected values, N variances, *and* $[N(N-1)/2]$ covariances. For any reasonably large number of N, few managers would be willing to estimate all these terms. In this case, Sharpe [1963] has offered an ingenious alternative approach. Suppose the rate of return on the ith security is to be estimated by the following regression equation:

$$r_i = a_i + b_i I + e_i$$

where I represents the rate of return on a market index (e.g., Dow-Jones or Standard & Poor), a_i and b_i represent the regression coefficients, and e_i represents the error term. Then[14]

$$E(r_i) = a_i + b_i E(I) \tag{12}$$

$$V_i = b_i^2 V_I + V_{e_i} \tag{13}$$

$$\text{COV}_{ij} = b_i b_j V_i \tag{14}$$

Thus we are able to reduce the enormous task of estimation to a manageable magnitude: we have only to obtain the regression parameters a_i, b_i, and V_{e_i}, and estimate $E(I)$ and V_I. These values would, in turn, provide the necessary values for our portfolio problem. Of course, this simplification is achieved at a cost: we lose pertinent information about

[13] The covariance between the ith and j^{th} securities is defined by

$$\text{COV}_{ij} = r_{ij}(V_i V_j)^{1/2}$$

where r_{ij} = the correlation coefficient. Hence, if one of the variances is 0, the covariance will also be 0.

[14] In regression analysis, it is assumed that

1. $E(e_i) = 0$
2. $V_{e_i} = C_i$, a constant
3. $\text{COV}_{e_i,I} = 0$
4. $\text{COV}_{e_i,e_j} = 0$

interrelationships reflected in the covariance terms. Whether the end result is *net* efficiency is a moot point.[15]

One conceptual issue is pertinent for our purposes. The portfolio model assumes that before the end of the period (periods), no liquidation of securities will be required. Although this objection would be specious in a multiperiod portfolio analysis,[16] even these attempts fail to take into account the transfer costs associated with liquidation of securities before their maturity.[17]

IV. Conclusion

In this chapter, we have investigated cash-management models that concentrate primarily on cash and marketable securities. Two approaches have been suggested in literature for this purpose. One avenue is the inventory-theoretic approach. Because the option exists for investing in more than one security, an extension of the inventory theory dealing with more than two assets is cumbersome. Moreover, the assumption of non-negative demand no longer holds for purposes of cash management; hence, the conventional inventory approach has little to offer on this subject. The other approach has been along the lines of the portfolio theory. This approach covers more than two assets; however, it fails to reflect the liquidity needs of the firm, the nature of the transfer costs, and the maturity structure of the marketable securities in the model, and thereby ignores their impact on the optimal holding of various securities and cash.

Appendix[1]

In the Miller–Orr model, cash-balance behavior is depicted in the following manner:

1. Cash balances are affected by uncontrollable transactions of one unit each with probability p that the cash balance will increase and q that it will decrease.

[15] Empirical evidence on this matter is inconclusive. See Francis and Archer [1971, pp. 96–107] for a more detailed analysis.

[16] For a dynamic version, see Mossin [1968].

[17] An extension of the portfolio theory incorporating varying transfer-cost components has been carried out by Jen and Zionts [1969]. However, their assumption of nonsymmetric transfer costs (i.e., no cost for transferring cash into securities, but a positive cost for the reverse process) does not sound plausible. Moreover, their use of a one-period model does not allow them to reflect the interrelationship among cash-balance behavior over time, transfer costs, and the maturity structure of securities that are typically considered by the manager in a nonfinancial corporation. Note that transfer costs (or rates of return) do not exhibit an invariant relationship with the maturity structure of marketable securities—even the government obligations. Thus we cannot use transfer cost as a surrogate for the maturity of a security. Implicitly, Jen and Zionts also assume liquidation of securities at the end of the period without cost, if they have not *already* been liquidated.

[1] This appendix is based on analysis by Orr [1970].

2. Cash balances are allowed to fluctuate in the above fashion between the lower limit 0 and the upper limit h.
3. When the cash balance reaches either of these extreme values, securities are bought and sold in such a way as to bring the cash balance to z units.
4. $$p = q = \frac{1}{2}$$

We want to determine (a) $P(T)$, the probability of security transactions in any *unit* period, and (b) $E(M)$, the *average* cash balance, given the above characterization of cash-balance behavior.

Suppose that during a given period we have had n transactions. Then, upon consummation of the $(n+1)^{\text{th}}$ transaction, the probability that the cash balance will be exactly x units is given by the expression

$$P_{n+1}(x) = pP_n(x-1) + qP_n(x+1)$$

That is, the cash balance was $(x-1)$ units, and the $(n+1)^{\text{th}}$ transaction brings the balance up to x units; *or* the cash balance was $(x+1)$ units and the $(n+1)^{\text{th}}$ transaction causes the outflow of one unit. When we multiply the appropriate probability, we get the above expression.

However, there is one important exception to that expression: the cash balance can be z units after the $(n+1)^{\text{th}}$ transaction if:

1. The opening balance before $(n+1)^{\text{th}}$ transaction was $(h-1)$ units, and the $(n+1)^{\text{th}}$ transaction brings the balance to h units, inducing a purchase of securities worth $(h-z)$ units.
2. The opening balance was 1 unit and the $(n+1)^{\text{th}}$ transaction brings it to 0 units, inducing a sale of securities worth z units.
3. The opening balance was $(z-1)$ units, and the $(n+1)^{\text{th}}$ transaction involves an inflow of 1 additional unit.
4. The opening balance was $(z+1)$ units, and the $(n+1)^{\text{th}}$ transaction results in the outflow of 1 unit.

In brief, when $x = z$

$$P_{n+1}(z) = pP_n(h-1) + pP_n(z-1) + qP_n(z+1) + qP_n(1)$$

In a compact form, we can write the following expression:

$$\left.\begin{aligned} P_{n+1}(x) &= pP_n(x-1) + qP_n(x+1) \quad \text{for } x \neq z \\ P_{n+1}(z) &= p[P_n(h-1) + P_n(z-1)] + q[P_n(z+1) + P_n(1)], \\ &\qquad\qquad\qquad\qquad\qquad\qquad \text{for } x = z \end{aligned}\right\} \quad \text{(A-1)}$$

Now, by definition, the *opening* balance (or the closing cash balance after the security transaction, if any) can be neither h nor 0. Therefore, this balance must be in some other state having a value between 0 and h. Thus

$$P_n(0) = P_n(h) = 0$$

and

$$\sum_{x=0}^{h} P_n(x) = \sum_{x=1}^{h-1} P_n(x) = 1$$

When n, the number of uncontrollable transactions, is very large, substituting the value $(p = q = \frac{1}{2})$, we can restate equation (A-1) in the following form:

$$\left.\begin{aligned} &P_{x-1} - 2P_x + P_{x+1} = 0, && x \neq z \\ &P_{z-1} - 2P_z + P_{z+1} + P_1 + P_{h-1} = 0, && x = z \end{aligned}\right\} \qquad \text{(A-2)}$$

As Goldberg [1958, Chapter 2, especially p. 57] has shown, these are difference equations, whose solution takes a linear form: i.e., the probability of being in the state x (having a cash balance of x units) is a linear function of x. Thus

$$P_x = A + Bx$$

Since $P(0) = P(h) = 0$, a trivial and unacceptable solution will be

$$A = B = 0$$

In order to avoid this nonsensical solution, we define

$$\left.\begin{aligned} &P_x = A + Bx, && 0 \leq x \leq z \\ &P_x = C + Dx, && z \leq x \leq h \end{aligned}\right\} \qquad \text{(A-3)}$$

Now $P(0) = 0$ implies that $A = 0$. Similarly $P(h) = 0$ implies that $C = -Dh$. Similarly, at z, both solution conditions hold; as a result

$$D = Bz/(z - h)$$

Since the sum of all probabilities is 1,

$$\sum_{0}^{z} Bx + \sum_{z}^{h} (-hD + Dx) = 1$$

or

$$B\sum_{0}^{z} x + D\left[\sum_{0}^{h} x - \sum_{0}^{z} x\right] - (h - z)hD = 1$$

i.e.,

$$(B - D)\frac{z(z + 1)}{2} + D\left[\frac{h(h + 1)}{2} - (h - z)h\right] = 1$$

Substituting the value for D, we get

$$-\frac{Bh}{(z-h)}\cdot\frac{z(z+1)}{2}+\frac{Bz}{(z-h)}\cdot\left[\frac{h(h+1)}{2}-(h-z)h\right]=1$$

or: $$\frac{Bzh}{2}=1$$

or: $$B=2/zh$$

Then $$P_x=\begin{cases}2x/zh, & 0\leq x\leq z\\ [2/(h-z)][1-x/h], & z\leq x\leq h\end{cases}\qquad\text{(A-4)}$$

Now in order to find the average balance, we have to derive the value

$$\sum_0^h xP_x$$

Thus, $$\sum_0^z x\left(\frac{2}{zh}x\right)+\sum_z^h x[C+Dx]$$

or: $$\frac{2}{hz}\sum_0^z x^2+\frac{2}{(h-z)}\left[\sum_0^h x-\sum_0^z x\right]-\frac{2}{h(h-z)}\left[\sum_0^h x^2-\sum_0^z x^2\right]$$

The above form is reduced to

$$\left(\frac{2}{hz}+\frac{2}{h(h-z)}\right)\sum_0^z x^2$$

$$+\frac{2}{(h-z)}\cdot\frac{(h+z)(h+z-1)}{2}-\frac{2}{h(h-z)}\sum_0^h x^2$$

Since $$\sum_0^z x^2=\frac{z(z+1)(2z+1)}{6}$$

we get:

$$\frac{1}{(h-z)}\cdot\frac{(z+1)(2z+1)}{3}+\frac{(h-z)(h+z-1)}{(h-z)}-\frac{(h+1)(2h+1)}{3(h-z)}$$

or $$E(M)=\sum_0^h xP_x=\frac{(h+z)}{3}\qquad\text{(A-5)}$$

As to the probability of transfer *during a given period,* we first note that a transfer would take place only if (1) the cash balance is 1 and the next transaction reduces it to zero, *or* (2) the cash balance is $(h-1)$

and the next transaction brings it to the upper limit h. For (1) the probability is

$$qP_1 = \frac{1}{2} P_1$$

For (2) the probability is

$$pP_{h-1} = \frac{1}{2} P_{h-1}$$

Because there are n transactions in a period,

$$P(T) = n \left[\frac{1}{2} P_1 + \frac{1}{2} P_{h-1} \right]$$

or:

$$P(T) = \frac{n}{z(h - z)} \tag{A-6}$$

7

Cash Management and Working Capital: Integration through Programming Approaches

I. Introduction

In Chapter 6, one major weakness of the analytic optimization models for cash management was noted: these models treat cash in a narrow framework of managing marketable securities. The conventional notion of the "cash cycle," however, requires a broader perspective for cash management. Hence, this chapter will deal with cash as an integral part of working-capital management. Such an integration requires specification of the interrelationships among various components of working capital. In the ordinary course of business, for instance, depletion of the finished-goods inventory implies an increase in either cash or accounts receivable, depending upon the credit-extension policy of the firm. Furthermore, the life span of the components of working capital interacts with two major activities of the firm: sales and production. Thus, what we require is to specify interrelationships among

1. Working-capital components
2. Sales and production activities and working capital

For this purpose, a linear-programming framework is utilized in this chapter. This approach does not directly provide *general* characteristics of the optimal solution; instead, it gives the optimal *numerical* solution upon specification of parameters in numerical terms. Its advantage lies in its flexibility, which will be evident in the treatment of the subject in this chapter. The second section deals with the goal of wealth maximization under deterministic conditions; the third section deals with the introduction of risk; and, the final section takes up the issue of multiple goals.

II. Wealth Maximization and Certainty

In a linear-programming approach, the relationships among the variables under observation are linear. The formulation of a problem in a linear-programming framework requires specification of an objective function that can be achieved within a set of constraints, which may be equalities or inequalities. Furthermore, the variables to be determined are nonnegative.

This formulation is generally stated in the following manner:

Maximize

$$\sum_i c_i X_i$$

subject to

$$\sum_i a_i X_i \leq b_i$$

and

$$X_i \geq 0$$

Here a_i, b_i, and c_i are parameters whose values are constant and known. X_i represents the decision variables whose values are to be determined.

In this section, we assume the goal of wealth maximization for the purpose of planning allocation of resources among different components of working capital. We shall first explore the nature of the constraints and then devise the objective function, with the help of the following example.

A. Statement of the Problems

A firm manufactures two products, X and Y. The manager of the firm is interested in liquidity planning for the next two weeks. The first week has five working days and the second week has four days. Each working day has an eight-hour shift.

The firm has 200 machines that can be used for production of both X and Y. A unit of product X takes 10 hours of machine time, whereas a unit of product Y takes 16 hours. Sales of product Y cannot exceed 800 units during the next 2 weeks.

Sales price, wages to labor, and costs of raw material per unit of X and Y are given below.

	X	Y
Sales price	$55	$125
Labor	30	48
Raw materials	10	50

Wages are paid in the same week as production; raw materials are bought on credit of one week and delivered immediately.

All sales are on credit, and payments are received one week from the day of sale.

Salary of the manager is $200 per week; it is not affected by the scale of operations.

The balance sheet at the beginning of the planning period is given in Table 7–1.

TABLE 7–1

Balance Sheet of . . . Company on December 1, 1969

Assets		*Liabilities and Equity*	
Cash	$ 2,000	Accounts Payable	$ 9,500
Marketable Securities	600	Bank Loans	7,500
Accounts Receivable	32,000	Current Liability	$17,000
Inventories	2,000	Long-Term Debt	22,500
Current Assets	$36,600	Net Equity	47,100
Fixed Assets	50,000		
Total Assets	$86,600	Total Liabilities & Equity	$86,600

As a matter of policy, the firm has maintained inventories of $2,000 in parts of some obsolete models. The current balance of marketable securities is earmarked for the tax payments. Furthermore, the firm maintains the minimum cash balance of $500. Finally, the company has an open credit line of $7,500 from a local bank; in order to preserve a favorable picture of the firm's financial situation, the manager believes that the "quick ratio" should not drop below 2.0.

B. Constraints

The constraints dealt with here are of two types: physical constraints and policy constraints. Physical constraints cannot be violated under any circumstances; for example, it is impossible for a given machine to produce more than a certain number of units in a day. On the other hand, policy constraints are imposed by management on the basis of either subjective considerations or considerations that cannot be adequately accommodated in the scope of this discussion. For instance, even though a machine can be worked for twenty-four hours a day, management may consider the capacity of the machine in terms of, at most, only eight hours a day because of problems of maintenance, supervisory control, and morale. We will designate *physical* constraints by numbers such as (P1) and (P2), and policy constraints by (M1) and (M2). The purpose of this distinction will be made clear in the subsequent sections.

Constraints will be formulated here in terms of *activities* of sales and production, working-capital *components* of cash,[1] and asset forms defining the quick ratio.

1. SALES

Let

X_1 = the optimal number of physical units of X to be produced (and sold) in the *first* week

X_2 = the optimal number of physical units of X produced in the *second* week

Y_1 = the corresponding number of physical units of Y produced and sold in the *first* week

Y_2 = the number of physical units of Y produced and sold in the *second* week

Then the statement of the problem suggests that

$$Y_1 + Y_2 \leq 800 \qquad \text{(P1)}$$

and

$$X_1, X_2, Y_1, Y_2 \geq 0 \qquad \text{(P2)}$$

2. PRODUCTION

The total hours of machine capacity available in each week puts an upper bound on production. For each of the 200 machines, the first week has 40 hours and the second week has 32 hours. Hence the total number of machine hours is 8,000 for the first week and 6,400 for the second week. Since a unit of X takes 10 machine hours and a unit of Y takes 16 machine hours,

$$10X_1 + 16Y_1 \leq 8{,}000 \qquad \text{(M1)}$$

$$10X_2 + 16Y_2 \leq 6{,}400 \qquad \text{(M2)}$$

3. CASH BALANCE

Cash outflows for any period, when adjusted for the non-negative beginning balance, cannot be larger than the cash inflows adjusted for the minimum balance. A positive minimum balance would be a policy

[1] For a linear programming formulation involving other components of working capital and interdivisional transfers, see Mehta and Inselbag [1973].

variable assumed to be known. In our case the minimum balance is \$500.

Cash *inflows* in each week are provided by collections of the accounts receivable representing sales of the previous week. In the first week, collections will be

$$\$32{,}000.$$

Similarly, collections in the second week will be

$$55X_1 + 125Y_1$$

Cash *outflows* result from (1) wages to labor of the current period, (2) purchases of raw materials in the previous period, and (3) salaries to managers in the current period. Thus, cash outflows of the first week will be

$$30X_1 + 48Y_1 + 9{,}500 + 200$$

Similarly, during the second week, cash outflows will be

$$30X_2 + 48Y_2 + 10X_1 + 50Y_1 + 200$$

Now the *beginning cash balance* in the first period is \$2,000. The beginning balance of the second week is provided by the sum of the beginning cash balance of the previous (first) period and the *net* cash flows of the same period. Thus, this quantity will be

$$2{,}000 + 32{,}000 - (30X_1 + 48Y_1 + 9{,}700)$$

i.e.,

$$24{,}300 - 30X_1 - 48Y_1$$

The cash-balance constraint for each of the two weeks will be as follows:

Cash outflows $\leq$ beginning balance + inflows − minimum balance

Thus, for the first week,

$$30X_1 + 48Y_1 + 9{,}700 \leq 2{,}000 + 32{,}000 - 500$$

or

$$30X_1 + 48Y_1 \leq 23{,}800 \qquad \text{(M3)}$$

For the second week,

$$30X_2 + 48Y_2 + 10X_1 + 50Y_1 + 200 \leq (24{,}300 - 30X_1 - 48Y_1) + 55X_1 + 125Y_1 - 500$$

or

$$-15X_1 - 27Y_1 + 30X_2 + 48Y_2 \leq 23{,}600 \qquad \text{(M4)}$$

4. QUICK RATIO

The quick-ratio[2] constraint will be given by

$$\frac{\text{Cash} + \text{marketable securities} + \text{accounts receivable}}{\text{Accounts payable} + \text{bank loans}} \geq 2.0$$

Cash balance at the end of the first week (or the beginning of the second week) is given by

$$24{,}300 - 30X_1 - 48Y_1$$

For the end of the second week, the quantity will be

$$24{,}100 + 15X_1 + 27Y_1 - 30X_2 - 48Y_2$$

Marketable securities are at the constant level of \$600 for each of the two weeks. Similarly, the bank loans are at the constant level of \$7,500.

Accounts receivable at the end of the first week will be

$$55X_1 + 125Y_1$$

The corresponding amount for the second week will be

$$55X_2 + 125Y_2$$

Accounts payable reflect purchases of raw materials. Hence,

$$10X_1 + 50Y_1$$

and

$$10X_2 + 50Y_2$$

will represent accounts payable for these two weeks respectively.

Thus, the quick-ratio constraint for the first week will be

$$24{,}300 - 30X_1 - 48Y_1 + 600 + 55X_1 + 125Y_1 \geq 2.0(10X_1 + 50Y_1 + 7{,}500)$$

or

$$-5X_1 + 23Y_1 \leq 9{,}900 \qquad \text{(M5)}$$

and for the second week

$$24{,}100 + 15X_1 + 27Y_1 - 30X_2 - 48Y_2 + 600 + 55X_2 + 125Y_2 \geq 20X_2 + 100Y_2 + 15{,}000$$

or

$$-15X_1 - 27Y_1 - 5X_2 + 23Y_1 \leq 9{,}700 \qquad \text{(M6)}$$

[2] If we wish to use the "current" ratio in place of the quick ratio, we have only to add inventories to the numerator on the left side of the constraint.

In brief, our problem has two physical constraints (P1 and P2) and five policy constraints (M1 to M6).

C. The Objective Function

Our objective is profit maximization.[3] Managerial salary is not affected by the choice of a planning alternative in the short run, so profit maximization is equivalent to maximization of the contribution margin on sales of X and Y. On product X the contribution margin is \$15; on Y, \$27. Thus our objective function will be

$$15X_1 + 15X_2 + 27Y_1 + 27Y_2$$

D. The Solution Procedure and Its Characteristics

We can now describe our problem as follows:
Maximize

$$15X_1 + 15X_2 + 27Y_1 + 27Y_2$$

subject to

$$10X_1 + 16Y_1 \leq 8{,}000 \quad \text{(M1)}$$

$$10X_2 + 16Y_2 \leq 6{,}400 \quad \text{(M2)}$$

$$30X_1 + 48Y_1 \leq 23{,}800 \quad \text{(M3)}$$

$$-15X_1 - 27Y_1 + 30X_2 + 48Y_2 \leq 23{,}600 \quad \text{(M4)}$$

$$-5X_1 + 23Y_1 \leq 9{,}900 \quad \text{(M5)}$$

$$-15X_1 - 27Y_1 - 5X_2 + 23Y_2 \leq 9{,}700 \quad \text{(M6)}$$

$$Y_1 + Y_2 \leq 800 \quad \text{(P1)}$$

$$X_1, X_2, Y_1, Y_2 \geq 0 \quad \text{(P2)}$$

We will not describe here the mechanics of the solution procedure.[4] Instead, we will assume that computer programs are available for the solution of the problem. For our problem, the computer program provides the following values:

---

[3] For our simple problem, the difference between profit maximization and wealth maximization is insignificant. When the analysis is extended to a number of equal-length periods encompassing a remote planning horizon, it is worthwhile to discount cash flows *and* the value of the assets at the horizon. When periods are of unequal length, as Orgler [1969] has postulated, the discount rate should reflect the appropriate duration of each period and those periods preceding the relevant period. Parenthetically, although Orgler's assumption is more realistic, it does not involve a significant conceptual distinction.

[4] For a lucid description of the Simplex Method (the prevalent solution procedure), and an economic rationale for it, see Baumol [1965], Chapter 5.

Variable	Optimal Value
X_1	77.6 units
X_2	75.7 units
Y_1	447.3 units
Y_2	352.7 units
Profit	$5,500.00

The computer program also provides the values for "dual" variables or "shadow prices" of the related constraints. A dual value represents the contribution to the objective function by a resource unit added to the existing relevant constraint. We have the following dual value for some related constraints:

Constraint	Dual Value
Machine Hours (M1)	0
Machine Hours (M2)	1.5
Cash Balance (M3)	0.5
Cash Balance (M4)	0
Quick Ratio (M5)	0
Quick Ratio (M6)	0
Sales of Y (P1)	3.0

Thus, if we have available $1 of extra cash in the first week (M3), this will contribute $0.50 of *additional* profit; however, an additional dollar in the second week (M4) does not make any contribution to the profit. Similarly, if somehow we can increase the machine hours by 1 unit in the second week, this will increase the profit by $1.50 in that week. Some implications of this interpretation may now be suggested. If we can borrow an additional dollar at the interest cost of less than 50 percent, borrowing it is worthwhile only during the first week. Furthermore, given the "unevenness" of the contribution of the additional dollar, the firm may find it advantageous to negotiate with the bank for an "average" ceiling of $7,500 instead of the present ceiling for *each* of the two periods, because in that case the firm may be able to profitably transfer some funds from the second period to the first period.

In brief, then, the dual variables have implications for policy in terms of the *right side* of the constraints. To the extent that constraints are policy matters or institutional restrictions, these dual variables measure the "costs" of these policies or restrictions. It should be noted here that these costs are truly *opportunity costs* in an economic sense. Thus each of them reflects the direct and indirect impact of a unit change in the related constraint on the objective measure through a maze of complex interrelationships. What is more important, this *net* impact is derived from considering a *change* to the *new optimal level* of all (directly and indirectly) related decision variables as a result of this unit change in the constraint. In this sense, then, dual variables are also measures of the "sensitivity" of the constraints. In a sensitivity analysis, of course, we vary the coefficients on the *left side* of the constraints and measure the impact of these variations on the objective function. In the dual analysis, as was noted above, sensitivity analysis is carried on by the dual formulation of the problem in the neighborhood of the values on the *right side* of the constraints. This sensitivity analysis of the constraint values and of the coefficients is particularly important for the deterministic framework presented here, because they provide ranges within which parameters may vary without seriously affecting achievement of the goal.

Nevertheless, it is obvious that the sensitivity analysis is deficient in handling situations involving uncertainty or risk because it does not *explicitly* encounter uneven probabilities for each of the possible outcomes within a range. We will now turn to the issue of accommodating uncertainty in the linear-programming framework.

III. Linear Programming and Uncertainty

Although we set our problem in a deterministic framework, some variables are partially exogenously determined and their absolute values are unknown. For example, whereas sales and collections from credit sales can be influenced indirectly through advertising expenditure and collection measures, they are, in practice, stated in terms of ranges and associated probabilities rather than absolute values. In such cases, relevant *policy* constraints are best stated in terms of probabilities. We now take up the method of handling such constraints. For this purpose, let us restate the constraint (M5) in general terms as

$$\text{Quick ratio [accounts payable + bank loans]} - \text{accounts receivable} \leq \text{cash + securities}$$

Suppose, for convenience, that collections are the only random variable. As a result, the outstanding accounts receivable and cash balance will be the random variables. Since other variables will be nonrandom, define

$$K = \text{Quick ratio } (A\text{-}P + \text{bank loans}) - \text{securities}$$

where K is a constant to be determined.

Now we will write (M5) in the following form:

$$\text{Prob } (\text{cash} + A\text{-}R - K \geq 0) \geq \alpha \qquad (1)$$

where α is a predetermined probability level, say, .99. This constraint indicates that, on the average, the quick ratio should not be below the minimum value 99 out of 100 times. If we now replace (cash + A-R − K) with a random variable $\tilde{L}$, we can restate the above inequality constraint as

$$\text{Prob}\ (\tilde{L} \geq 0) \geq \alpha$$

or

$$\text{Prob}\ (\tilde{L} \leq 0) \leq 1 - \alpha,$$

assuming that L has a continuous distribution.

Replace $(1 - \alpha)$ by β. Thus

$$\text{Prob}\ (\tilde{L} \leq 0) \leq \beta \tag{2}$$

or

$$\text{Prob}\left\{\left(\frac{\tilde{L} - E(L)}{S(L)}\right) \leq -\left(\frac{E(L)}{S(L)}\right)\right\} \leq \beta$$

where $E(L)$ is the expected value of $\tilde{L}$ and $S(L)$ is the standard deviation. Our purpose is to turn this probabilistic constraint, better known as a "chance contraint," into a certainty-equivalent constraint. We shall utilize here the Tchebycheff inequality,[5] which states that

$$\text{Prob}\left(\frac{\tilde{L} - E(L)}{S(L)} \leq \lambda\right) \leq \frac{1}{1 + \lambda^2}, \qquad \lambda < 0 \tag{3}$$

Equivalently,

$$\text{Prob}\ (\tilde{L} \leq E(L) + \lambda S(L)) \leq \frac{1}{1 + \lambda^2} \tag{4}$$

A comparison between expressions (2) and (4) indicates that the former expression satisfies the constraint in the form of (4), if

$$\beta = \frac{1}{1 + \lambda^2} \tag{5}$$

and

$$E(L) + \lambda S(L) \geq 0 \tag{6}$$

From (5), and given $\lambda < 0$, we get

$$\lambda = -\left[\frac{1 - \beta}{\beta}\right]^{1/2}$$
$$= -\left(\frac{\alpha}{\beta}\right)^{1/2}$$

[5] The method suggested here differs from that of Charnes, Cooper, and Symonds [1958], who employ the notion of *linear decision rules* for certainty-equivalent constraints. The approach here is an adaptation of a discussion by Starr and Miller [1962], pp. 64–66.

Thus, we can write the constraint (6) in the following form:

$$E(\text{cash}) + E(A\text{-}R) - K - \left(\frac{\alpha}{1-\alpha}\right)^{1/2} S(L) \geq 0 \tag{7}$$

Now finding the value $S(L)$ requires not only the standard deviations of cash and accounts receivable but also the covariance between them —K, being a constant, has the standard deviation 0. One still stronger form of inequality is possible in this case.

By definition,

$$\text{Var}(L) = \text{Var}(\text{cash}) + \text{Var}(A\text{-}R) + 2 \cdot \text{COV}(\text{cash}, A\text{-}R)$$

or

$$[S(L)]^2 = [S(\text{cash}) + S(A\text{-}R)]^2 - 2 \cdot S(\text{cash}) \cdot S(A\text{-}R)[1 - r(\text{cash}, A\text{-}R)]$$

where $r(\text{cash}, A\text{-}R)$ is the correlation coefficient between cash and $A\text{-}R$. Hence,

$$S(L) \leq S(\text{cash}) + S(A\text{-}R) \tag{8}$$

Inserting this ceiling value of $S(L)$ in (7), we get

$$E(\text{cash}) + E(A\text{-}R) - K - \left(\frac{\alpha}{1-\alpha}\right)^{1/2} [S(\text{cash}) + S(A\text{-}R)] \geq 0$$

Thus a knowledge of the expected value and standard deviation of random components as well as the threshold probability level enables us to convert the chance-constraint into a certainty-equivalent form.

It should be noted here that the chance-constrained method can be applied only for converting *policy* constraints into chance-constraints, because *physical* constraints, by definition, cannot be violated, and hence their probabilistic form will be meaningless. Now, if only *policy* constraints can be chance-constraints, it follows that their dual evaluators would be a function of the prescribed threshold probability level. These dual evaluators are, then, the *implicit costs* of policy constraints. When we explicitly consider costs of policy constraints, we follow the method of goal programming described in the next section.

IV. Goal Programming[6]

In the standard linear-programming formulation, the distinction between physical and policy constraints has no meaning. In chance-constrained programming, policy constraints amenable to probabilistic formulation are found to have implicit costs. In either case, however,

[6] The discussion in this section has benefited from the lucid presentations by Mao [1969] and Ijiri [1965].

management hierarchy of goals cannot be undertaken directly or conveniently. For instance, in the standard linear-programming formulation, our goal is wealth maximization subject to policy constraints such as minimum cash balance and quick ratio. In this sense management has three goals:

1. Wealth maximization
2. Minimum cash balance
3. Quick ratio

Because the constraints have to be met for an optimal feasible solution, the goals embodied in (2) and (3) will *always have a priority* over wealth maximization. Now it may be possible that management wants to have a minimum cash balance of $100,000 under *normal* circumstances but would gladly live with an $80,000 cash balance if it meant an increase in profit of $50,000. Under the standard formulation, the only clue we might have as to this profit potential comes from the dual variables. In turn, since dual variables are connected with the optimal solution, it is only by trial and error that we decide upon $80,000 of cash balance. This is at best an indirect, if not inconvenient, method of establishing a hierarchy of goals. Furthermore, the standard formulation treats all constraints with equal weights. This is appropriate for physical constraints; but, so far as policy constraints are concerned, management may have a distinct priority. Again, in the above case, management may be concerned more with the quick ratio than with the minimum cash balance. In this case, even chance-constrained programming does not provide any direct help. Finally, different constraints have different directional motivations, and the previous linear-programming formulations cannot reflect them adequately. For example, management likes to have at least the minimum cash balance in all periods, but at the same time it frowns upon a large excess balance over this minimum amount. Thus large deviations in either a positive or a negative direction are undesirable. We can certainly accommodate this objective by placing upper and lower limits on the cash balance. However, the desirability of turnover ratios is unidirectional: although they should not fall below a minimum value, their larger value is desirable. In the standard formats considered earlier, this desirability cannot be explicitly built into the model.

These considerations have led to the development of goal programming. Its basic premise is that policy constraints embody managerial goals, with a hierarchy and directional desirability (in addition to their target values) known to management. Goal programming requires the reformulation of the policy constraints and the objective function.

A. Policy Constraints

Here we shall discuss two constraints: cash flow (M3) and quick ratio (M5), which are restated in an abbreviated, generalized form:

$$\text{Opening cash bal}_t + \text{cash inflow}_t - \text{cash outflow}_t \geq \text{min cash}_t$$

and
$$\text{Liquid assets}_t - \overline{QR}\ (\text{current liability})_t \geq 0$$

where t refers to the time period and $\overline{QR}$ is the desired quick ratio. First, these inequality constraints are converted into equalities by introducing dummy variables.[7] Thus the first constraint becomes

$$\text{Opening cash bal}_t + \text{cash inflow}_t - \text{cash outflow}_t$$
$$- \text{min cash}_t - C_t^+ + C_t^- = 0$$

where C_t+ represents "surplus" above the minimum cash balance and C_t- represents "deficit" below this balance. For any feasible solution only one of these numbers, at most, will be positive. If, for a particular optimal solution, the excess over the minimum cash balance is, say, $5,000, C_t+ will have the value, 5,000, and C_t- will have the value 0. Only then can the equality be maintained. Of course, *both* C_t+ and C_t- can be zero; this will happen when the projected balance is exactly equal to the minimum balance.

Similarly, the second constraint becomes

$$\text{Liquid assets}_t - \overline{QR}\ (\text{current liability})_t - Q_t^+ + Q_t^- = 0$$

As a second step, a third constraint is added to our original set of constraints. What was originally the objective function is now turned into another constraint. Suppose that W represents the original objective function, and that the *target* value of discounted cash flow is $\overline{W}$, according to management plans. Then, the additional constraint would be:

$$W - \overline{W} - W^+ + W^- = 0$$

Again, $W+$ would connote overachievement of the target, and $W-$ would connote a shortage in the target.

The question is: What is our objective function? We will now turn to this issue.

B. The Objective Function

Suppose that management has prepared the following table of priorities of three goals:

---

[7] These dummy variables differ from the conventional ones used by the computational methods (e.g., the Simplex Method) in one important way: they play a crucial role in formulating the objective function, as we shall see below.

		Attitude toward	
Goal	Priority	Overachievement	Underfulfillment
Wealth	1	Desirable	Undesirable
Quick ratio	2	Moderately desirable	Undesirable
Cash balance	3	Indifferent	Mildly undesirable

The entries in this table are interpreted as follows. Management assigns top priority to the goal of wealth maximization. It would like to see the target exceeded by planned results and would not be in favor of falling short of this target. On the other hand, it assigns the lowest priority to cash balances, and would not be either concerned or overjoyed if planned cash balances exceed the minimum cash balance, so long as the excess is not negative. Of course, if cash balances fall short of the "minimum" balance, management would tolerate the situation only if it has a justification, say, in terms of increased profitability.

The purpose of the tabular set-up is to determine (1) a hierarchy of goals and (2) the extent (and direction) of deviation from targets, which is deemed undesirable. This facilitates the next task: assigning *penalties* to deviations. In the above case, we may assign P_1 to W^+, P_2 to W^-, . . . , P_5 to C^+, and P_6 to C^-. From our reasoning it is clear that $P_5 = 0$ because excess cash balances do not concern us. On the other hand, P_2 will be a positive coefficient, say, .25. At the same time, P_1 would be a negative coefficient, say, $-.10$. Once we have assigned these penalty numbers, we are able to construct our objective function:

$$\text{Minimize } P_1W^+ + P_2W^- + P_3Q^+ + P_4Q^- + P_5C^+ + P_6C^-$$

Our objective function thus minimizes deviations from targets for different goals. When deviations are desirable, the penalties are negative—i.e., they represent "rewards"—and when deviations are undesirable, the penalties are positive. When there is indifference toward deviations, penalties are nil. Our assignment of the value of $(-.10)$ to P_1 and (.25) to P_2 thus indicates that management encourages positive deviations from the target goal of wealth, but assigns a penalty of \$0.25 to each dollar by which the goal is underfulfilled.

In brief, the goal-programming procedure requires the following modifications in the standard linear-programming formulation:

1. Convert *policy* constraints into equalities by introducing dummy variables[8] for positive and negative deviations from target values.
2. Convert the original objective function into an equality in the same fashion.

[8] Naturally, these variables are non-negative.

3. Determine the hierarchy of goals and assign penalties in the form of numerical weights to positive and negative deviations from the targets of different goals.
4. Utilize the penalties and variables representing deviations in formulating the objective function that calls for minimization (maximization) of penalties (rewards) associated with undesirable (desirable) deviations.

Once these modifications are completed, the optimal solution can be computed in the same fashion as for any standard linear-programming problem.

It should be noted here that the actual numbers assigned as penalties to deviations are much less important than the hierarchy of goals they represent. This notion is particularly important for a multiple-goal situation involving conflicting goals. For example, an increase in inventory turnover may be accomplished by a smaller receivables turnover ratio, and vice versa. If management assigns a very heavy penalty to one ratio and a relatively small penalty to the other, it is likely to achieve improvement in one number at the cost of deterioration in the other. In a standard linear-programming format, both goals would have been constraints, and their conflicting nature would not have been brought out at the planning stage. In the goal-programming approach, on the other hand, management has to decide early in the game whether a particular goal has any priority over another goal, and to what extent.

V. Conclusion

In this chapter, cash was viewed as an integral part of the management of working capital. The format of linear programming was employed for cash management in this sense. Initially, the goal of discounted cash flow was considered for a multiperiod planning problem under deterministic conditions. Subsequently, a chance-constrained approach was suggested to account for risk or uncertainty in the problem. Finally, a goal-programming formulation was presented in order to accommodate a variety of complementary or conflicting goals that are typically encountered in working-capital management.

Cash as a Residual Asset and Simulation

I. Introduction

CHANGES in cash balance do not occur solely as a result of interactions among the components of working capital. There are also transactions that do *not* originate from activities associated with working-capital components but still affect cash balances: capital expenditures, dividend payments, and long-term debt servicing are the obvious examples. These transactions possess characteristics distinct from those of the working-capital components. In the first place, although these transactions are infrequent, their individual impact is great because of the size of each individual transaction. Second, they are often unpredictable. At the same time, they are controllable only in the long run, and often their flexibility is asymmetrical. For instance, dividend payments are typically associated with earnings. Dividend payments in the future will not be certain because future earnings cannot be predicted with certainty. Moreover, since management generally reduces the dividend amount only reluctantly (and often only as a last resort),[1] dividend payments have flexibility only in the upward direction. Similarly, capital expenditures depend on such factors as obsolescence and the need for expansion. These factors are unpredictable; but when

[1] cf. Lintner [1956].

they do occur, postponement of capital expenditure is only a theoretical possibility and would hardly be a sound operational strategy. In brief, the finance manager cannot effectively manage cash balances without considering these infrequent but consequential transactions, which are not necessarily either predictable or controllable.

When these transactions are predictable but uncontrollable, approaches such as programming frameworks can still handle them with ease. For instance, debt servicing is predictable with certainty, and its impact would be to reduce available funds for each future period, individually and cumulatively. When transactions are unpredictable but controllable, we may use their expected value as a surrogate for predictable, certain value, and accommodate them in the programming framework. However, when these transactions are both unpredictable and uncontrollable (not in the legal sense, but from the strategic viewpoint), programming frameworks become awkward because risk is not adequately reflected in the expected value. Furthermore, the individual categories of transactions are not necessarily independent; hence, in order to determine their *net* impact on cash balances, convolution of probability distributions of these interrelated variables is necessary. For instance, the probability distribution of future dividends is affected by the probability distribution of earnings, which in turn is determined by probability distributions of sales and cost. In a similar way, the probability distribution of future capital expenditures depends upon the distribution of obsolescence and that of expansion needs affected by sales. Moreover, to the extent that capital expenditures are *primarily* financed through retained earnings, distributions of capital expenditures and dividends (representing the difference between earnings and retained earnings) are not only indirectly related through sales but also directly related through the availability of funds.

The task of formulating convoluted probability distributions of interrelated variables, even when it is feasible, is either extremely complex or prohibitively expensive. Consequently, simulation is often resorted to as an expedient method for developing such joint, convoluted probability distributions. For cash management in the long run, simulation is expedient as well as effective because transactions affecting cash balances not only are related *within* a period but also have interrelationships *across* periods.

In this chapter, the nature and structure of the simulation process will be first described. Then the Monte Carlo method, a specific simulation technique for handling uncertainty, will be explained. Finally, the usefulness of simulation in decision making for cash management will be explored.

II. Simulation

A. Characteristics

A *system* is a configuration of logical interrelationships among relevant elements. The notion of relevancy here depends upon the purpose or purposes for which a system is constructed: what is relevant for one purpose may be irrelevant for another. Cash management succinctly illustrates this view. Under the programming approach, when the planning horizon is relatively short, cash inflows from an investment about to be undertaken may not be relevant. When, on the other hand, cash flows are to be analyzed for determining cash inadequacy during future recessions, the impact of cash flows generated by an imminent investment cannot be safely ignored.

Simulation is basically an experimental, numerical method that enables us to study the impact of a series of changes in an element (or set of elements) upon other elements in the system.[2] Thus, in order to carry out simulation, specification of the system should be such that the system can be subjected to *numerical* manipulation. The experiments performed on the system are *artificial* in the sense that they may not necessarily have a counterpart in reality.

Basically, simulation is undertaken for the following two reasons:

1. To obtain insights into the functioning of the system by postulating relationships.
2. To design an optimal system (when some elements are controllable and the relationships are known but complex) that leads to a set of desired goals such as cost minimization and wealth maximization.

In the first case, analytical relationships are postulated. Through simulation, outcomes are generated, and their pattern is verified in the light of observed (or observable) reality. Suppose we are interested in finding out the impact of different prices for a new product on the total realizable sales revenue. On a very simple level, this will require knowledge of the elasticity of the demand function relating prices to quantity of output sold. In addition, however, we have to take into account the substitution effect of the new product on demand for other products sold by the firm. Furthermore, we have to postulate the capacity of different categories of *credit* customers to absorb the output of the new product at different price levels, and the ability of these customers to pay for the credit. If we have (1) not omitted any relevant variables, (2) not included superfluous variables in our system, (3) formulated the functional relationships accurately, and (4) estimated the numerical values of the relevant coefficients within a reasonable range, simulation of the system should provide us with valuable insights into the impact of introducing a new product on the cash inflow. For example, we may conclude from such a study that the introduction of a new product in some well-entrenched lines is not worthwhile, even when the new product is technically far superior to comparable existing products; on the other hand, in some other lines, creating a new "image" for an existing product, as through advertising campaigns,

---

[2] For a detailed treatment of simulation, see Naylor and Vernon [1969].

would have a significantly favorable impact on the generation of cash flows.

The second purpose, the design of an optimal system, presumes that functional relationships are known and that their coefficients can be affected by some policy actions. These systems are complex and their overall formulation prevents application of analytical techniques in order to reach generalized solutions. For example, direct-cost saving is anticipated upon installation of new machines in place of existing ones. However, the optimal output level for new machines may be large enough to require larger distribution expenditure as well as higher collection and bad-debt costs. Even programming techniques prove to be inadequate in this case because *coefficients* of the funds constraints (such as the collection cost or bad-debt cost for the amount collected) do not remain constant. If we are to treat them as constant, we are likely to reach conclusions different from those warranted by a sound policy.

In how much detail should we establish the functional relationships? As with the case of relevant elements, the answer primarily depends on the purpose for which simulation is being carried out. It also depends on the planning horizon. If our objective, for example, is to gain insights into alternative long-term strategies of the firm, the planning period may be ten or fifteen years in the future, and the relationships will necessarily be relatively general in scope. Thus, we may not be seriously concerned about the precise *timings* of cash flows associated with credit sales. On the other hand, if our purpose is to determine the worst possible cash-level outcome during a number of hypothetical recession periods, we cannot safely ignore the relationship between accounts receivable and cash flow. Other considerations, such as cost, computer capacity, and program efficiency, also affect the desirable level of details in the simulation procedure.

So far we have discussed the simulation process (presumably in a multiperiod setting) on the assumption that the relationships between individual components are deterministic. When they are *not* deterministic, a *heuristic* procedure may be applied: such a procedure involves consideration of only *reasonable* alternatives. For instance, we may decide that the worst possible sales decline in a particular period cannot be more than 20 percent, and that sales growth would not exceed 25 percent in a given period. Thus, alternatives related to sales growth exceeding 25 percent and sales declines any larger than 20 percent are ruled out. A commonplace example of heuristics is the consideration of three possible outcomes that may or may not be equally likely: most optimistic, realistic, and most pessimistic.

For purposes of cash management, even when functional relationships are known, the numerical values of coefficients (parameters) over time do not remain unchanged. One consequence of this characteristic is that simulation will not provide us with *optimal* policies; at best, it will enable us to gain valuable insights. Furthermore, given the uncertainty about the values of the parameters, we can use the deterministic form of simulation only as an approximation of reality. However, when a probability distribution of each relevant element is provided, the behavior of cash balances over time can be studied more effectively through the Monte Carlo method than through such deterministic approximations.

B. The Monte Carlo Method

The Monte Carlo method, rather than being defined, will be illustrated by means of two examples, which will enable us to delineate its characteristics and requirements.

Suppose that our planning horizon is two periods and the probability is 4/10 that in *one* period we will run out of cash under a given strategy. We want to determine the overall probability (over two periods) for each of three mutually exclusive possibilities of running out of cash: not at all, once in two periods, and in both periods. Initially, for convenience, let us assume that the surplus or the deficit of the first period is not carried forward to the second period.

It is certainly possible to solve this problem theoretically. However, we will suggest here the solution procedure of the Monte Carlo method. Suppose we have 10 chips, numbered consecutively from 1 to 10, in a jar. Drawing any one of the chips numbered 1, 2, 3, and 4 is, then, the equivalent of running out of cash. A chip with a number from 5 to 10 will be the equivalent of having adequate cash. Suppose we draw a chip once, record the result, replace the chip in the jar, and draw a chip again. This process then will "simulate" one *trial* experiment of running out of cash in a two-period time span. When we repeat this procedure for a large number of trials, our record will show the number of frequencies for (1) not running out of cash at all, (2) running out of cash once, and (3) running out of cash in both periods. If we turn these absolute numbers of frequencies into *relative* frequencies by dividing the first by the total number of trials, it will be reasonable to equate relative frequencies with the desired probability distribution.

If the probability of running out of cash in *one* period were, say, 0.356, we would need 1,000 chips numbered consecutively from 1 to 1,000; and drawing a chip containing a number from 1 through 356 would correspond to the event of running out of cash.

Now let us admit the assumption of cumulative cash balances. In this case, it is necessary to define the probability distribution of all possible cash levels. Suppose that in an individual period cash cannot fall below -2 units and cannot exceed $+3$ units as a result of transactions during the period. For two periods, we find that at the *end* of the second period, the cash balance may indicate a deficit level of -4 units (-2 units in each of the two periods), a surplus level of $+6$ units, or any intermediate value. Similarly, for three periods, the lowest level will be -6 units and the maximum level will be $+9$ units. In general, for n periods, the lowest level will be $-2n$ and the maximum, $+3n$. We would like to determine the probability corresponding to each of the $(5n + 1)$ cash balance levels. Suppose that we are provided with the following probability estimates for changes in cash balance during *one* period:

Level, x	Probability, $f(x)$
−2	.10
−1	.12
0	.30
+1	.32
+2	.16

These probabilities can be easily converted into *cumulative* probabilities. Thus:

Level Not Exceeding x	Cumulative Probability, $F(x)$
−2	.10
−1	.22
0	.52
+1	.84
+2	1.00

If we now "draw" a random number from the list containing 1 to 100, we associate numbers 1 through 10 with the level −2, numbers 11 through 22 with the level −1, and so on. We can repeat the process n times (for n periods), and record the *cumulative* sum of the drawing for each period. This now constitutes a trial, and the cumulative level constitutes an event. When we have run a large number of trials, we derive the desired probability distribution for each period in the same fashion as before, by determining the relative frequency of each possible event, the cash level.

From the above description of the Monte Carlo method, it is possible to pinpoint the following requirements for the procedure:

1. Parameters of the systems should be quantifiable.
2. There should be an adequate supply of "random" numbers. That is, all numbers within a specified range should have equal probability of being chosen.[3] In practice, prepared tables of random numbers are available.[4]
3. The basic probability distribution of the relevant element should be

[3] In practice, randomness is often tested through the weak test of serial correlation: i.e., correlation between a pair of two consecutively drawn numbers should be zero.

[4] Cf. Rand Corporation [1955]. Since such a table occupies an excessive space in a computer, pseudo-random number-generating algorithms have also been developed: e.g., Meyer [1956], especially the article by O. Taussky and J. Todd.

available. In the above case, for instance, we had the one-period probability distribution for changes in the cash level, and from that we were able to derive the corresponding multiperiod distributions.

So far we have described only one variable, net cash-level changes in one period. This variable may be decomposed into a number of other variables, as is shown in Table 8–1. For the purpose of deriving the

TABLE 8–1

Transactions	Related Elements
Sales	*Market Size*
	Market Growth Rate
	Market Share
	Price
	Quantity
	Bad-debt Expense
Operating Cost	*Labor Wages*
	Raw Materials
	Price-level Changes
	Productivity Changes
	Production Volume
	Cost of Goods
Fixed Cost	*Administrative Staff Size*
	Salaries
	Advertising Expenditures
	Collection Expense
	Depreciation Expense
	Interest Expense
Taxes	Earnings before Taxes
Debt Servicing	Interest Charges
	Sinking-fund Obligations
Capital Expenditure	Expansion
	Obsolescence
	New Products
Dividends	Earnings before Taxes
	Taxes

changes in cash level, we need to know the distributions of the items under the heading "Related Elements" that are *underlined.* The solution procedure will now require a random selection of each of these elements, which will then be combined appropriately to yield the changes in cash level. When this procedure is repeated several times, we derive the desired probability distribution.

One modification is often called for in the above procedure of deriving a distribution based on multiple elements. Sometimes, two or more elements are related. In such cases, we need to specify these relationships. Suppose that we are interested in projecting capital-expenditure distribution that results from obsolescence and from development of new products. When obsolescence is perceived to be imminent, replacement expenditures may be postponed, and research and development (R&D) efforts may be stepped up. This increased R&D activity may mean increased construction expenditures three or four years from now. Thus, additional construction expenditures are *partially* conditioned by previous R&D expenditures, which, in turn, may *coincide* with obsolescence. If we divide the obsolescence rate into three categories—little, normal, and abnormally high—we need to define the distribution of R&D expenditures for these three categories separately, and from those distributions we can derive the probability distribution of construction expenditures.

Although the concept of developing conditional distributions is straightforward, its implementation is by no means easy in a multiperiod context, because the number of conditional (secondary) distributions increases rapidly with the number of periods. In such instances, heuristic procedures, dealing with only *reasonable* alternatives, are applied to keep the task manageable.

III. Simulation and Decision-making: Concluding Remarks

Once we have developed the desired probability distribution or distributions (one- or multi-period, and cumulative or noncumulative) through simulation, our next task is to utilize this information for decision making. Of course, the nature and details of this information set are clearly conditioned by the purpose, as we have seen above. But we will now take up a few examples related to cash management to link the product of simulation to decision making.

In this chapter, we have treated cash as a residual of all assets and transactions. The basic implication of this premise is that cash management cannot be optimized without due regard to repetitive as well as infrequent transactions affecting cash balances. One likely motivation of cash management from this viewpoint is: Do we have enough cash balances during the entire planning period to meet reasonable eventualities? What the finance manager is required to do is to determine which eventualities are reasonable for him. The probability distribution or distributions developed by simulation allow him to define "reasonableness" more precisely: if the cumulative probability is below a certain predefined level, the occurrence of the minimum level is deemed unreasonable. For example, the manager regards one chance in 100 as barely reasonable. If the cumulative probability is .01 for a cash level of $10,000, he would draw the conclusion that under reasonable circumstances the cash balance will not drop below $10,000. Of course, he may define, as an alternative, a minimum cash balance, say, of $45,000. If the cumulative probability of a cash balance as high as $45,000 is .05, he would have to decide whether one chance in 20 of living with a cash balance lower than $45,000 is acceptable. Thus simulation allows the manager to determine either the minimum level or the reasonable eventuality of cash inadequacy once he specifies one of these two parameters, and thereby determine cash adequacy during the planning period.

Once the manager has determined whether or not there is a reasonable chance for cash inadequacy, he may take an appropriate course of action. For example, when cash balances are anticipated to be inadequate, he may decide to take one or more of the following actions:

1. Do nothing, and live with cash inadequacy.
2. Negotiate with a bank for a larger line of credit.
3. Monitor more closely inventories of the products with high unit values.
4. Tighten credit extension during the upturn of the business cycle.
5. Increase dividends by a smaller amount.
6. Postpone capital expenditures or cut the size of the capital budget during the initial period of recovery, when the demand for cash is particularly critical.
7. Restructure the debt maturity so as to avoid two or more balloon payments within a short period.

It should be noted that when there is more than one planning period, the cash balances will be cumulative in nature. Furthermore, the manager will be concerned with cash inadequacy during *each* of the planning periods.

When we are concerned with the problem of liquidity for determining the debt capacity of the firm,[5] we still deal with cash inadequacy. However, this case differs from the above in one crucial respect: now we are concerned with cash adequacy during *adverse* periods. This problem is not only likely to require additional information in the form of a more refined probability distribution for the lower tail of the distribution but also will demand more detailed information during the entire length of *recession* or adverse circumstances.

Simulation also enables us to develop useful information for evaluating alternative investment strategies. Cash-flow distributions developed for this purpose need not be in great detail. As a matter of fact, if the portfolio analysis suggested by Markowitz is pertinent, all we require is estimation of periodic cash flows in the form of the expected value, variance, and covariances over time. In such a case, our concern is with conversion of the cash-flow distributions into certainty-equivalent values that are based on these estimates.

When dividend policies are being determined, cash-flow simulations are particularly helpful. Earlier we have referred to the aversion of management to changes in dividend policy that require reduction in the amounts of dividends. Inadequacy of cash balances is one condition leading to this unpleasant policy decision. Management may avoid such a step by not increasing dividend amounts in earlier periods to the extent embodied in the simulation.

[5] See Donaldson [1961].

There are many such applications dealing with simulation as applied to cash management; the list above is by no means comprehensive. What is important is that simulation does not interpret cash management in the narrow sense of inventories, where the only controllable element is the purchase or sale of securities. Nor does it restrict cash management to being a nexus of decisions related to other components of working capital and sales and production activities, as was the case with the programming models. Finally, it allows us to account for risk in its complex form.

At the same time, simulation by itself is not able to provide optimal policies because the functional relationships among various components are not known with certainty and do not remain constant over time. Still, insights gained through simulation are certainly helpful in making strategy decisions and are likely to pave the way to more general analytical models.

References

Baumol, William J., "The Transactions Demand for Cash: An Inventory Theoretic Approach," *Quarterly Journal of Economics,* November 1952, p. 135.

———, *Economic Theory and Operations Analysis* (2nd ed.). Englewood Cliffs, N.J.: Prentice-Hall, Inc., 1965, fn. 156.

Beckman, Theodore N., *Credits and Collections, Management and Theory* (7th ed.).New York: McGraw-Hill Book Company, 1962, fn. 12.

Beranek, William, *Analysis for Financial Decisions.* Homewood, Ill.: Richard D. Irwin, Inc., 1963, fn. 40, p. 47.

———, *Working Capital Management.* Belmont, Cal.: Wadsworth Publishing, 1966, fn. 4.

Bierman, Harold and Alan K. McAdams, *Management Decisions for Cash and Marketable Securities.* Ithaca, N.Y.: Graduate School of Business, Cornell University, 1962, p. 135.

Boot, Johannes C. G., *Mathematical Reasoning in Economics and Management Science.* Englewood Cliffs, N.J.: Prentice-Hall, Inc., 1967, fn. 89.

Buchan, Joseph and Ernest Koenigsberg, *Scientific Inventory Management.* Englewood Cliffs, N.J.: Prentice-Hall, Inc., 1963, fn. 95.

Burton, John C., *Credit Management for Maximum Profit.* New York: Arthur Young & Co., 1965, fn. 24.

Charnes, A., W. W. Cooper, and G. H. Symond, "Cost-Horizons and Certainty Equivalents: An Approach to Stochastic Programming of Heating Oil," *Management Science,* April 1958, fn. 159.

Cyert, R., H. Davidson, and G. Thompson, "Estimation of the Allowance for Doubtful Accounts by Markov Chains," *Management Science,* April 1962, pp. 40 & 47.

Donaldson, Gordon, *Corporate Debt Capacity*. Boston: Division of Research, Graduate School of Business Administration, Harvard University, 1961, fn. 173.

Eppen, Gary and Eugene Fama, "Solutions for Cash Balance and Simple Dynamic Portfolio Problems," *Journal of Business,* January 1968, p. 136, fn. 140.

———, "Cash Balance and Simple Dynamic Problems with Proportional Costs," *International Economic Review,* June 1969, p. 136, 139.

Francis, Jack C. and Stephen H. Archer, *Portfolio Analysis*. Englewood Cliffs, N.J.: Prentice-Hall, Inc., 1971, p. 145.

Goldberg, Samuel, *Introduction to Difference Equations*. New York: John Wiley & Sons, 1958, p. 147.

Hadley, George and Thomson Whitin, *Analysis of Inventory Systems*. Englewood Cliffs, N.J.: Prentice-Hall, Inc., 1963, fn. 72, fn. 119.

Howard, Ronald A., *Dynamic Programming and Markov Process*. Cambridge, Mass.: Technology Press, 1960, fn. 39, fn. 124.

Ijiri, Yuji, *Management Goals and Accounting for Control*. Chicago, Ill.: Rand McNally, 1965, fn. 160.

Jen, Francis and Stanley Zionts, "Effects of Liquidity Risk on Portfolio Selection," *Working Paper,* State University of New York at Buffalo, 1969, fn. 145.

Lintner, John, "Distribution of Income of Corporations among Dividends, Retained Earnings, and Taxes," *American Economic Review,* May 1956, fn. 165.

Magee, John F., "Decision Trees for Decision Making," *Harvard Business Review,* July 1964, fn. 36.

———, "How to Use Decision Trees in Capital Investment," *Harvard Business Review,* September 1964, fn. 36.

Mao, James C. T., *Quantitative Analysis of Financial Decisions*. New York: Macmillan & Co., 1969, fn. 160.

Markowitz, Harry M., *Portfolio Selection: Efficient Diversification of Investments*. New York: John Wiley & Sons, 1959. Cowles Foundation Monograph #16, p. 142.

Massé, Pierre, *Optimal Investment Decisions*. Englewood Cliffs, N.J.: Prentice-Hall, Inc., 1962, fn. 5, fn. 36.

Mehta, Dileep R., "The Formulation of Credit Policy Models," *Management Science,* October 1968, fn. 27.

———, "Capital Budgeting Procedures for a Multinational Firm," in R. Holton and S. P. Sethi (ed.) *New Perspectives in International Business*. New York: Free Press, 1974, fn. 5.

Mehta, Dileep and Isik Inselberg, "Working Capital Management of a Multinational Firm,' in S. P. Sethi and J. N. Sheth (ed.) *Multinational Business Operations: Financial Management*. Pacific Palisades, Calif.: Goodyear Publishing Company, Inc., 1973, fn. 153.

Meyer, H. A., ed., *Symposium on Monte Carlo Methods*. New York: John Wiley & Sons, 1956, fn. 170.

Miller, Merton H. and Daniel Orr, "A Model of the Demand for Money by Firms," *Quarterly Journal of Economics,* August 1966, p. 136.

Modigliani, F. and Merton H. Miller, "The Cost of Capital, Corporation Finance, and the Theory of Investment," *American Economic Review,* June 1958, fn. 5.

———, "Corporate Income Tax and the Cost of Capital: A Correction," *American Economic Review,* June 1963, fn. 5.

Morgan Guaranty Trust, *Money Market Investments.* New York: Morgan Guaranty Trust, 1964, fn. 142.

Mossin, Jan, "Optimal Multiperiod Portfolio Policies," *Journal of Business,* April 1968, fn. 145.

Naddor, Eliezer, *Inventory Systems.* New York: John Wiley & Sons, 1966, fn. 72, fn. 81.

Naylor, Thomas H. and John M. Vernon, *Microeconomics and Decision Models of the Firm.* New York: Harcourt, Brace, & World, 1969, fn. 167.

Neave, Edwin H., "The Stochastic Cash Balance Problem with Fixed Costs for Increases and Decreases," *Management Science,* March 1970, p. 140.

Orgler, Y. E., "An Unequal Period Model for Cash Management Decisions," *Management Science,* October 1969, p. 156.

Orr, Daniel, *Cash Management and the Demand for Money,* New York: Praeger Publishers, 1970, p. 134, fn. 140, fn. 145.

Rand Corporation, *A Million Random Digits with 100,000 Normal Deviates.* Glencoe, N.Y.: The Free Press, 1955, fn. 170.

Resek, R., "Uncertainty and the Precautionary Demand for Money," *Journal of Finance,* December 1967, p. 135.

Sastry, A. S. Rama, "The Effect of Credit on Transactions Demand for Cash," *Journal of Finance,* September 1970, p. 135.

Schlaifer, Robert, *Probability and Statistics for Business Decisions.* New York: McGraw-Hill Book Company, 1959, fn. 23.

Sharpe, William F., "A Simplified Model for Portfolio Analysis," *Management Science,* January 1963, p. 144.

Smith, P. F., "Measuring Risk on Consumer Credit," *Management Science,* November 1964, p. 15.

Solomon, Ezra, *The Theory of Financial Management.* New York: Columbia University Press, 1963, fn. 4.

Sprenkle, Case, "Is the Precautionary Demand for Money Negative?" *Journal of Finance,* March 1970, p. 135.

Starr, Martin K. and David W. Miller, *Inventory Control.* Englewood Cliffs, N.J.: Prentice-Hall, Inc., 1962, fn. 72, fn. 76, fn. 96, fn. 97, fn. 100, fn. 118, fn. 159.

Tuttle, D. and R. Litzenberger, "Leverage, Diversification, and Capital Market Effects on a Risk Adjusted Capital Budgeting Framework," *Journal of Finance,* June 1968, fn. 5.

Wagner, Harvey M., *Statistical Management of Inventory Systems.* New York, N.Y.: John Wiley & Sons, 1962, fn. 129.

Weston, John F. and Eugene F. Brigham, *Managerial Finance.* New York: Holt, Rinehart & Winston, 1972, fn. 12.

Whalen, E. L., "An Extension of the Baumol-Tobin Approach to the Transactions Demand for Cash," *Journal of Finance,* March 1968, p. 135.

Williams, Evan J., *Regression Analysis.* New York: John Wiley & Sons, 1959, fn. 16.

Index

Acceptance cost, 21, 23, 24–25, 51–55, 59–63
Accounts receivable management, 9–67
  collection measures, 33–49
  credit granting, 11–32
  credit policy integration, 50–67
Acid-test ratio, 6
Archer, Stephen H., 145*n*

Bad-debt ratio, 13
Baumol, William J., 135, 156*n*
Bayes theorem, 20, 21
Beckman, Theodore N., 12*n*
Beranek, William, 4*n*, 46*n*, 47, 48, 49
Bierman, Harold, 135
Boot, Johannes C. G., 89*n*
Brigham, Eugene F., 12*n*
Buchan, Joseph, 95*n*

Carrying cost, 135
"Cash cycle," 2, 150
Cash management, 131–74
  of cash as a residual asset, 165–74
  and inventory theory, 135–41
  and marketable securities, 133–49
  and portfolio management, 141–45
"Chain investment," 36
Charnes, A., 159*n*
Collection:
  activities, 9
  expenditures, 65
  measures, 33–49
    application, 41–44
    Markov process and cash-flow estimates, 36–41
    selection of policy and capital budgeting, 34–36
Consumer credit, 10
Cooper, W. W., 159*n*
Cost of capital, 4, 5
Credit granting, 9, 11–32
  control measures, 27–31
    aggregate indices, 29–30
    sensitivity analysis, 30–31
    variables affecting, 28–29
  conventional approach:

Credit granting (*continued*)
    control measures, 13–14
    evaluation measures, 13
  decision-tree approach, 23–27
    evaluation, 27
    illustration, 24–26
    investigation process, 26–27
  discriminant analysis:
    cutoff value, 19–22
    evaluation, 22–23
    index construction, 17–19
    limitation, 31
    sample selection, 16–17
    significant factors, 15–16
Credit policy integration, 50–67
  control indices, 63–67
  cost estimates:
    acceptance cost, 51–55
    lost-sales cost, 55–57
  decision rules, 57–63
Credit turnover ratio, 13
Current assets:
  inventories reported as, 2
  See also Working capital
Current ratio, 6, 155*n*
Cyert, R., 40, 47

Davidson, H., 40, 47
Debt-equity ratio, 15–16
Decision tree, 23–27, 36, 63
Donaldson, Gordon, 173*n*
Dow Jones index, 142
Dun & Bradstreet, 13
Dynamic programming, 86–89

EOQ (economic-order-quantity) model, 73–91, 98, 102
  and cash balances, 135–36
    under uncertainty, 136–41
  inventory-sales relationships, 75–76
  ordering time, 76–77
  relaxation of assumptions, 77–91
    demand rate, 81–89
    lead time, 78–80
    quantity discounts, 89–91
  sensitivity analysis, 76
Eppen, Gary, 136*n*, 139, 140*n*

Fama, Eugene, 136*n*, 139, 140*n*
Fixed-order system (FOS), 101, 102–10, 117–18, 125–26, 127, 129
Fixed-period system (FPS), 101, 110–18, 126, 127, 129
Francis, Jack C., 145*n*

Goal programming, 160–64
Goldberg, Samuel, 147

Hadley, George, 72*n*, 119*n*
Heuristic procedure, 168
Howard, Ronald A., 39*n*, 124*n*

Ijiri, Yuji, 160*n*
Inselberg, Isik, 153*n*
Inventory cycle, 78, 111, 117, 120
Inventory management, 69–130
  under certainty:
    EOQ model, 73–91
    evaluation of inventory system, 98–100
    investment constraint, 93–96
    multi-item inventory, 91–93
    relevant costs, 72–73
    various items from one supplier, 96–98
  under uncertainty, 101–30
    comparison of FOS and FPS, 117–18
    control of multi-item inventories, 124–29
    (s,S) system, 118–24
    safety stock and FOS, 102–10
    safety stock and FPS, 110–17
Inventory theory and cash management, 135–41
Inventory turnover ratio, 6
Investment cost, 73

Jen, Francis, 145*n*

Koenigsberg, Ernest, 95*n*

Linear programming, 158–60
Lintner, John, 165*n*
Liquidity, 3, 173
Litzenberger, R., 5*n*
Lost-sales cost, 21, 55–57, 65, 73, 128, 129

McAdams, Alan K., 135
Magee, John F., 36*n*
Management practice, 5–6
Mao, James C. T., 160*n*
Marketable securities, 133–49
  distinguished from cash, 134
  inventory theory:
    EOQ model, 135–36
    under uncertainty, 136–41
  portfolio management, 141–45
Markov process, 36–41, 51, 53*n*, 102, 119–24
Markowitz, Harry M., 142, 173
Massé, Pierre, 5*n*, 36*n*
Mehta, Dileep, 5*n*, 27*n*, 153*n*
Meyer, H. A., 170*n*
Miller, David W., 72*n*, 76*n*, 96*n*, 97*n*, 100*n*, 118*n*, 159*n*
Miller, Merton H., 5*n*, 136–41, 145–46
Modigliani, F., 5*n*
Monte Carlo simulation, 129*n*, 166, 169–72
  requirements, 170–71
Morgan Guaranty Trust Company, 142*n*
Mossin, Jan, 5*n*, 145*n*

Naddor, Eliezer, 72*n*, 81*n*
Naylor, Thomas H., 167*n*

Orgler, Y. E., 156*n*
Orr, Daniel, 136–41, 145–46

Portfolio management, 141–45
Portfolio theory, 5, 134

Quick ratio, 152, 155–58, 161, 163

Rand Corporation, 170*n*
Randomness, 140
Receivable turnover ratio, 6
Rejection cost, 21, 23, 24–25, 59–63
Reorder point, 102–3
Research and development (R&D), 172
Resek, R., 135
Risk, 5, 9

(s,S) system, 101, 118–24, 127
Safety stock:
  and FOS, 102–10
  and FPS, 110–17
Sales forecasting, 3
Sastry, A. S. Rama, 135
Schlaifer, Robert, 23*n*
Sequential decision process, 23
Serial independence, 140
Setup cost, 72–73, 135
Sharpe, William F., 144
Shortage cost, 73, 103–4, 105–6, 116
Simplex Method, 162*n*
Simulation:
  characteristics, 166–69
  and decision making, 172–74
  Monte Carlo method, 169–72
  reasons for undertaking, 167
Smith, P. F., 15
Solomon, Ezra, 4*n*
Sprenkle, Case, 135
Stability, 140
Standard & Poor's index, 142
Starr, Martin K., 72*n*, 76*n*, 96*n*, 97*n*, 100*n*, 118*n*, 159*n*
Stationarity, 140
Storage cost, 103
Symonds, G. H., 159*n*
System, defined, 166

Taussky, O., 170*n*
Tchebycheff inequality, 159
Thompson, G., 40, 47
Todd, J., 170*n*
Trade credit, 10
Tuttle, D., 5*n*

U.S. government obligations, 1–2

Vernon, John M., 167*n*

Wagner, Harvey M., 129*n*
Wealth maximization, 151–58
Weston, John F., 12*n*
Whalen, E. L., 135
Whitin, Thomson, 72*n*, 119*n*
Williams, Evan J., 16*n*
Working capital:
activity levels, 3–5
asset forms, 3–5
and cash management, 150–64
characteristics, 1–5
components, 1, 131, 150
life span, 1–2
net, 1*n*

Zionts, Stanley, 145*n*